SEVEN
VISIONS

SEVEN VISIONS

IMAGES OF
—CHRIST—
IN THE DOCTRINE AND COVENANTS

Adam S. Miller | Rosalynde F. Welch

DESERET
BOOK

Salt Lake City, Utah

Visit us at deseretbook.com

Library of Congress Cataloging-in-Publication Data

CIP on file

ISBN 978-1-63993-339-6

Printed in the United States of America
Lake Book Manufacturing, LLC, Melrose Park, IL

10   9   8   7   6   5   4   3   2   1

For Melissa Wei-Tsing Inouye,
who trusted Christ's promise
and lived a life full of life

— CONTENTS —

INTRODUCTION

The Gospel of John recounts a lively episode in which Jesus debates Jewish authorities at the temple. You "search the scriptures," he tells them, "for in them ye *think* ye have eternal life," but "they are they which testify of me" (John 5:39; emphasis added). The scriptures are not an end in themselves, he teaches. They are only powerful witnesses of Christ and his kind of life, the kind of life Christ calls "eternal." His interlocutors, though, refuse to see the living source of all life standing there in their midst. But "ye will not come to me," Jesus laments, "that ye might have life" (John 5:40).

President Russell M. Nelson recently urged Latter-day Saints to seek Christ with efforts "ever more intentional." He asked: "What will happen as you more intentionally hear, hearken, and heed what the Savior has said and what He is saying now through His prophets?"[1]

This is good counsel and an important question.

As a people, we commonly strain our ears to "hear him" (Joseph Smith—History 1:17). We seek God's voice in scripture. But are we also intentional about seeking his face?

This is ultimately the goal: not only to hear Christ's voice but to see his face. As Elder Robert Daines put it, "We want to see Jesus for who He is and to feel His love." To see the face of Christ is one of scripture's great promises, but *what it means* to see his face is one of scripture's great puzzles. More than simply a vision of the Savior, seeing Christ begins with our being seen and transformed by him. But for this to happen, we must learn how to recognize his features—and, too, to recognize him as the light by which everything else is seen. When we see Christ, we see the love of the Father and we see the way back into his presence. This is the labor of discipleship, and as Elder Daines taught, "We're not finished until we see Jesus as the face of our Father's love and follow Him, not just His rules."[2]

Seeing the face of Christ is the work of a lifetime. In this work, the prophets—both ancient and modern—lead the way. Their objective is always the same. The objective is Christ. "Sanctify yourselves that your minds become single to God, and the days will come that you shall see him; for he will unveil his face unto you, and it shall be in his own time, and in his own way, and according to his own will" (Doctrine and Covenants 88:68). Could there be any more urgent pursuit than to find our way, sanctified and single-minded, back into the presence of God?

As the authors of this book, our hearts' desire is this—though, despite our devotion (and despite being, somehow, already more than midway through life), we remain novices in this pursuit.

Our search has, in many ways, run on parallel tracks. We grew up—on opposite coasts but with similarly fortunate childhoods in the Church—singing the Primary song "Tell Me the Stories of Jesus" and then, gradually, learning to read those stories about Jesus for ourselves. We served missions for the Church, bearing Christ's name as we took our first faltering steps into mature discipleship. Then, as disciple-scholars, we followed our respective inclinations into higher education—again on opposite coasts and again in parallel doctoral programs, one in philosophy and one in literature—and began, tentatively, to practice a kind of gospel scholarship we'd never quite seen before. We've worked for decades now, together and with a close group of colleagues, to develop methods of closely and faithfully reading our Restoration scriptures that also draw on the unusual tools of our scholarly disciplines. And along the way, for good measure, we've each married and raised children, bought houses, pursued careers, served in the Church, read countless books, wrote a few, and burned candles at both ends.

Life, now, is racing past. Some hopes have been realized, and some disappointments have been endured. But regardless of these relative gains and losses, we've had more than enough time to verify for ourselves that fundamental truth taught by every prophet: nothing but God can satisfy. And if we are to experience as fully as possible the sweetness of a life in Christ before we die, we must dedicate our lives, with urgency, to seeking his face here and now.

This book is one fruit of that search.

As disciples who are also scholars, we follow Elder Neal A. Maxwell's lead and call our work a form of "disciple-scholarship." Disciple-scholarship, at root, is the business of consecrating our academic skills for the work of better understanding the truths of the Restoration. In our case, scholarly training has given us a broad familiarity with the history of Western thought in general and Western philosophy and theology in particular, as well as the skills of slowly and carefully reading difficult texts. When it comes to interpreting scripture, these academic tools are, of course, useless unless paired with enduring conviction and wielded with persistent humility. And even then, this work's spiritual value depends entirely on the Spirit.

This is the measure for all disciple-scholarship: When the gospel is preached, do we "preach it by the Spirit of truth or some other way? And if it be by some other way it is not of God" (Doctrine and Covenants 50:17–18). And, too, when we receive this teaching, do we "receive it by the Spirit of truth or some other way? If it be some other way it is not of God" (Doctrine and Covenants 50:19–20).

Featuring a series of close readings and shared reflections on seven visions of Christ in the Doctrine and Covenants, this book is organized around two central ideas. The first is that the Doctrine and Covenants contains true accounts of modern, prophetic visions of Christ, and we suggest that reading these seven visions can become occasions for our own personal encounters with Christ. And, too, we suggest that a careful study of these visions can help us better understand *how* the veil is rent when these visions are given— and, thus, reveal how we, in our own ways, can better emulate these prophets in our search for Christ (see Doctrine and Covenants 110:1). Accordingly, we are not primarily interested in these visions for their historical value—for what they might reveal about the history of the Church or even the Prophet Joseph Smith's own personal history. Rather, we are almost exclusively interested in Christ. Our goal is to read these passages as sacred scripture and to stay attuned throughout to the immediate spiritual stakes of the truths conveyed.

The second idea that organizes this book is the conviction that the journey of seeking Christ's face in the Doctrine and Covenants should be shared. It should be collaborative. We cannot succeed alone, as Saints or disciple-scholars. As President Bonnie Cordon urged: "Come unto Christ and don't come alone."[3] Having collaborated closely as friends and colleagues—for many years now and on a wide variety of texts—we've found again and again that our most compelling and meaningful work always involves scripture. And we've also found that working together, rather than alone, greatly increases both the joy and the revelations that accompany any serious engagement with scripture. And, so, as with our previous book, *Seven Gospels: The Many Lives of Christ in the Book of Mormon*, we've structured this volume as a series of letters that offer careful readings of the texts of these seven visions, that put these various readings in dialogue with each other, and that openly and happily incorporate the intimate details of our own loves, fears, and personal experiences.

The Doctrine and Covenants is, among all our scriptures, a unique text. It is a compilation of extraordinary modern visions and revelations. Lacking an overarching narrative like the Book of Mormon, its revelations are also eclectic in occasion, genre, and subject matter. However, if there is a single theme that unites all 138 sections, we believe a strong case can be made that this theme is the Prophet Joseph Smith's quest to see the face of Christ.

And not Joseph alone. Joseph's First Vision, his translation of the Savior's visit to ancient peoples, his efforts to build the city of Zion, and his urgent work building houses of the Lord and revealing the ordinances that would usher his people into the presence of God—all of this revelatory work was motivated by a remarkable generosity of spirit that insisted that Joseph's access to God was not intended to be rare or unique. Rather, Joseph's prophetic mission was grounded in his desire to offer every Saint the opportunity to hear for themselves what he'd heard, to know for themselves what he knew, and to see for themselves what he'd seen.

While the revelations compiled in the Doctrine and Covenants take a wide variety of forms, from epistles to detailed visions to notes culled from sermons, the central revelation is always the same: the parting of the veil to reveal the person and character of Jesus Christ, the "Alpha and Omega, the beginning and the end, the light and the life of the world—a light that shineth in darkness and the darkness comprehendeth it not" (Doctrine and Covenants 45:7).

As the source of all true light in the cosmos, Christ "comprehended all things, that he might be in all and through all things, the light of truth; which truth shineth" (Doctrine and Covenants 88:6–7). Thus, to see Christ is both to behold his person *and* to begin to see everything else by his light. To see him, we must also

5

learn to see as he sees—to see the world as he sees it, through his eyes, from his perspective, with his perfect love.

Consequently, the seven visions we've selected include some of Joseph's best-known visionary experiences. But they also include some lesser-known sections that, just as surely, reveal crucial truths about the light of Christ. The seven visions studied here include:

- Section 19, Christ's account of his eternal atonement
- Section 45, the vision of Christ's second coming to the city of Zion
- Section 76, Joseph Smith and Sidney Rigdon's vision of Christ and the kingdoms of glory
- Section 88, the epic vision of Christ as the true light and law of the universe
- Section 110, Joseph Smith and Oliver Cowdery's vision of Christ in the Kirtland house of the Lord
- Section 130, the Prophet's promise that when Christ appears, we will see him as he is
- Section 138, Joseph F. Smith's vision of Christ among the dead

We could, of course, have focused on any number of other visions recorded in the Doctrine and Covenants. (And we encourage you to study those as well!) But for our purposes, we selected these seven revelations not only for their focus on Christ but because they also include some strong visual element. Each chapter of this book opens with a brief summary of the revelation we'll explore, both to refresh your memory of its overall shape and themes and to prime your focus on the vision of Christ at its center. While this set of revelations certainly includes descriptions of dramatic open visions of Christ in his heavenly glory, as with section 76 and section 110, this hasn't prevented us from sometimes using the term *visions* more broadly, as Elder Jeffrey R. Holland does, to refer to the centrality of Christ in any disciple's outlook: "To grasp the vision we are seeking, the healing that [Christ] promises, the significance we somehow know is here, we must cut through the commotion—joyful as it is—and fix our attention on Him."⁴ Visions of this kind result from training our spiritual eye on Christ, whether in response to a divine visitation or a verse of scripture.

Apart from this selection of topics, we did not begin writing this book with a predetermined outline in mind. We simply took each revelation as it came and began to recognize patterns and recurring themes only as they emerged. It's striking, then, that these seven visions yield such a unified witness. And it's striking that these visionary experiences result, again and again, from the same sets of circumstances.

The formula is flexible, of course, but repeatedly we see a prophet first immersed in scripture, pondering tough questions in the text and working to clarify, understand, and explain what is being said. And, again and again, we witness these prophetic figures working collaboratively, welcoming the input of loved and trusted friends. The often-shared visions that result are never treated as the private property of a spiritual elite but are instead offered freely to all as examples and encouragement. The account of each vision is animated by a conviction that _everyone_ is welcome to witness Christ and enter the presence of God.

Over the course of our work, it also became clear that a handful of biblical texts served as important conversation partners for these seven visions. The opening chapter of the Gospel of John echoes throughout the whole of the Doctrine and Covenants, as does John 14. In this respect, John's Gospel may be an essential companion when reading these visions. In addition, imagery from the book of Revelation is frequently entwined in the Doctrine and Covenants' portraits of Christ enthroned, as the Bridegroom and as Alpha and Omega. And lastly, the Savior's own apocalyptic teachings in

Matthew 24 and 25—especially its focal image of Christ descending in clouds of glory—often reappear in these visions.

Finally, we also found that a handful of urgent questions link these seemingly disparate visions: What is the glory of God, and how can we learn to bear this glory ourselves? What does it mean to dwell in and with Christ? And are we simply awaiting Christ's eventual return, or is he somehow already present in our midst?

We, of course, offer no definitive answers to these questions. Our work is scholarly and exploratory, not authoritative. We hope only that, having joined us, you'll be left with a strong desire to put the Prophet's methods to work in your own spiritual life. We hope you'll gain an appreciation for Joseph Smith's prophetic gifts and visionary generosity and that you'll regard his revelations of Christ as crowning additions to their biblical counterparts.

But most of all, we hope that these visions will kindle in your heart a longing to see the face of Christ.

We hope you'll come to feel as the Psalmist did—and as we ourselves have come to feel—when praying to God. We hope you'll pray, with all the energy of your soul, this very old but very powerful prayer: "When thou saidst, Seek ye my face; my heart said unto thee, Thy face, Lord, will I seek" (Psalm 27:8)!

Rosalynde Welch
Adam Miller

— CHAPTER 1 —

The Endless Christ

DOCTRINE AND COVENANTS 19

In this revelation, the Lord speaks to Martin Harris as Alpha and Omega, the Redeemer of the world, and the agent of the Father. Christ paints a vision of himself in Gethsemane, suffering and trembling because of pain and bleeding at every pore. He unfolds the mystery and divine meaning of *eternal* and *endless* punishment. The Lord's atoning suffering, which Martin will never know, was voluntarily accepted so that his people need not suffer if they repent.

Martin is commanded to impart a portion of his property for the printing of the Book of Mormon. He is instructed to not covet his own property or that of his neighbor. The Lord asks him to repent and learn of him, promising Martin that he will be blessed if he follows these commandments faithfully. Martin is invited to preach repentance, continue in meekness, pray always, and come unto the Savior.

Rosalynde,

Midway through life, I've been rethinking my failures—as a husband, as a father, as a disciple of Christ. I suspect that you, like me, are no stranger to this kind of navel-gazing.

For a long time I thought that, given my failures, I must be bad. Or, at least, that some vital parts of me must be bad. And when I failed, I failed because—why else?—I wasn't good enough to be good.

Certainly I'm a sinner, at least of an ordinary sort. And regardless of my reasons, I'm responsible for these failures. I'm accountable. I'm without excuse. After all, as Paul emphasizes, "there is none righteous, no, not one" (Romans 3:10). "Every man walketh in his own way, and after the image of his own god, whose image is in the likeness of the world" (Doctrine and Covenants 1:16). We all need Jesus to save us.

But rethinking my failures, I've come to disagree with this old assessment of my root problem. I think I've had, all this time, my causes and effects confused. I've had my order of operations muddled.

I may be bad in some ways—but this isn't just because I'm bad. It's because I've been wrong.

My root problem isn't badness but blindness. It's not evil but error.

I think I've been wrong in basic ways, for most of my life, about who God is and what God wants from me. I've ignored the substance of what God's prophets have asked me to believe. And, as a result, I've been wrong about even the most obvious things: about what, as a human being, I even am and then what, as a disciple, I've been trying to do.

As a sinner, I've suffered the problem Joseph Smith describes in section 123 of the Doctrine and Covenants. I've "inherited lies" and been colonized by a spirit of deception (123:7). And the resulting badness has been "urged on and upheld by the influence of that spirit which hath so strongly riveted the creeds of the fathers, who have inherited lies, upon the hearts of the children, and filled the world with confusion"—a spirit that's "been growing stronger and stronger, and is now the very mainspring of all corruption, and the whole earth groans under the weight of its iniquity" (123:7).

These lies, these deceptions—not some inborn badness—are the mainspring of my corruption. And the revelations canonized in the Doctrine and Covenants are intended as targeted antidotes for exactly this crippling infection.

If we take the above as a starting point, this argument also offers a handy way to mark, in broad strokes, what I take to be an important difference between the Book of Mormon and the Doctrine and Covenants.

Where the Book of Mormon's primary job is to confirm the fundamental truth of the Bible's vision of Christ—"proving to the world that the holy scriptures are true," as Doctrine and Covenants 20:11 says—one of the Doctrine and Covenants' principal jobs is to correct for key distortions that have crept into this received vision.

Not only does the Doctrine and Covenants confirm the biblical witness but it also boldly improves on that witness, calling us to see Christ more clearly than ever before.

Reading these modern revelations together, I suspect you and I will come back to this point again and again. Throughout these revelations, we'll witness God calling us to see and accept deep and surprising truths that reorganize the whole of what we, as Christians, thought we'd already understood.

For example, I think it's hard to overestimate the corrective value of section 76's revelation that there are three degrees of glory (not simply a heaven and a hell), section 130's revelation that God the Father also has a body of flesh and bones, or section 138's vision of Christ redeeming the dead. These revelations don't just amend a few tangential details here and there; they reframe the whole gospel of Jesus Christ. They project the biblical narrative against a wholly original backdrop and port familiar gospel principles onto an entirely different platform, rebooting those tried-and-true prophetic programs in the context of a novel operating system. This is the Restoration.

Imagine reading the Old Testament for the first time, as an early Christian, in light of the New Testament. Every well-known text would be lit by a flood of new light streaming in from unexpected angles.

The Doctrine and Covenants, I think, does a similar thing but for *all* our previous revelations. The Doctrine and Covenants is to the Bible and the Book of Mormon what the New Testament is to the Old. In one sense, things remain just as they were. All the previous revelations remain intact. But in another sense, things couldn't look more different than they had just a moment ago.

In this respect, the revelations gathered in the Doctrine and Covenants aim to reveal truths hidden from the foundation of the world (see Matthew 13:35). They aim to disclose what these revelations frequently call the mysteries of godliness. "For, behold," section 19 says, "the mystery of godliness, how great is it!" (19:10).

What, though, is this mystery of godliness? And how, if I catch this vision, could it help liberate me from those crippling errors, riveted on my heart by that spirit of deception? How might it cure my blindness?

Section 19 is, in my view, an astonishing revelation that (almost casually) unwinds thousands of years of Christian tradition with just a handful of verses that redefine what God means when he says "eternity."

"I will explain unto you this mystery," the Lord tells Martin Harris, "for it is meet unto you to know" (19:8).

The revelation was occasioned by Martin's growing anxiety about insuring the payment for the publication of the Book of Mormon. He was nervous that he could lose "essentially all the property to which he had legal right." Martin, distraught, repeatedly pled for guidance, and section 19 resulted.[5]

As given through Joseph Smith, the revelation breaks into two halves: (1) verses 1–19 dramatically revise the meaning of "eternal" punishment and culminate in an extraordinary, first-person description of God's own suffering on our behalf, and (2) verses 20–41 consist of detailed instructions for Martin that command him to stop "coveting," among other things, his own property and accept the fact that, to join God in this work, he'll need to sacrifice much more than just 150 acres.

Taken at face value, the two halves of the revelation don't appear to have much in common. But I think they're actually talking about the very same mystery: how we, as Christians, are meant to emulate Christ in our handling of loss and suffering.

The revelation opens by emphasizing how Christ is both the beginning and the end and then quickly narrows its focus to just the "end." At "the end of the world," on "the last great day of judgment," the Lord says, there will be "weeping, wailing and gnashing of teeth, yea, to those who are found on my left hand" (19:3, 5).

To be found on Christ's "left hand" on the day of judgment is bad news. As Jesus explains in Matthew 25:31–46, on the day of judgment, he'll separate the "sheep" from the "goats," placing the sheep on his right hand and the goats on his left. The sheep are blessed, and the goats are cursed.

What distinguishes the sheep on the right from the goats on the left?

The goats find themselves on the Lord's left hand because they were blind in mortality to God's present and pressing reality. God came to them in the form of suffering—in the form of the hungry, the thirsty, the naked, the prisoner—and they didn't respond to this suffering as if it were their own, meeting it with care and compassion. They were blind to the Lord's presence. "Lord, when saw we thee an hungred, or athirst, or a stranger, or naked, or sick, or in prison, and did not minister unto thee?" the goats will ask (Matthew 25:44). Jesus, though, will answer them, "Verily I say unto you, Inasmuch as ye did it not to one of the least of these, ye did it not to me" (Matthew 25:45).

If he fails to repent, Martin will be like these goats. He'll continue to be blind. He'll continue to "run about . . . as a blind guide" (Doctrine and Covenants 19:40). Or he'll be like those who continue to look "for a Messiah to come who has already come" (19:27).

Goats, then, are defined by the fact that they're blind to God's presence. They continue to look for God somewhere else, someway else, sometime else—when God is *already* here.

This is understandable—who hasn't acted similarly?—but blindness is still blindness.

Refusing to repent, we've all failed to connect with God as he's most commonly manifest in the world. We've all failed to see that God, the greatest, is already given and available in "the least of these," because "inasmuch as ye have done it unto one of the least of these my brethren, ye have done it unto me" (Matthew 25:40).

This blindness to God's presence, to the fact that he's hidden in plain sight, is mirrored, I think, in our blindness to the true nature of eternity.

And it's here, with respect to the question of "eternity," that section 19 makes its most powerful and surprising amendment to the broader Christian tradition.

Those who are found on the left hand of God will, the Lord says, suffer "endless torment," just as we've always been told. But—and here's the real thunderbolt—this does *not* mean that their torment will never end. "It is not written that there shall be no end to this torment" (19:6).

Why, then, is it called "endless" or "eternal" if it will have an end?

Two reasons are given.

The first reason is pragmatic.

"It is written *eternal damnation*" so that it is "more express than other scriptures, that it might work upon the hearts of the children of men, altogether for my name's glory" (19:7). In short, it's called "endless" or "eternal" to grab our attention and incentivize repentance.

The second reason, though, is substantial.

Promising to "explain unto [us] this mystery," the Lord adds that this punishment is also called "endless" or "eternal" because "I am endless, and the punishment which is given from my hand is endless punishment, for Endless is my name. Wherefore—Eternal punishment is God's punishment. Endless punishment is God's punishment" (19:8, 10–12).

In one sense, "eternal" punishment is hyperbole, a rhetorical flourish meant to soften our hearts, because this punishment will ultimately have an end. But in a much more important sense, the Lord explains, "eternal" punishment, even if it ends, really *is* still eternal—it's just that we've been wrong about what eternity means.

Given our blindness, we've defaulted to seeing eternity as a kind of future-tense *quantity* when, fundamentally, eternity is more like a present-tense *quality*. Or we might say: eternity is less like an endless *when* and more like an immediate *how*.

As one of God's names, *eternity* describes how God works in the world. It describes how God himself handles loss and suffering, error and evil—how he refuses to "shrink" in the face of life's troubles and, instead, greets these troubles with selflessness, charity, and compassion (see 19:18).

Whenever life's suffering is greeted in this way—in God's way, in the Eternal One's way—with steady, unflinching, redemptive compassion—then eternity obtains. Eternity is realized.

Here, eternal life is God's kind of life and rather than being an escape from time or something beyond time, "eternity" seems to name a divine dimension *of* time, a qualitatively divine way of handling time, that cares for and redeems time, even as time continues to flow.

This may be surprising, but it's surprising in the same way Matthew 25 is surprising. It's surprising in the same way that, inasmuch as we've loved the least among us, we've already successfully loved the greatest. And inasmuch as we've handled the losses and suffering of ordinary time as God does, then time has already been successfully redeemed.

When this happens, when time is redeemed, then time is "full" of eternity, "pressed down, and shaken together, and running over" (Luke 6:38). The fulness of time has arrived and there's no need to continue looking forward "for a Messiah to come" when he "has already come" (Doctrine and Covenants 19:27).

The urgent question this leaves us with is this: if eternity is more like a quality than a quantity, then what kind of life *does* God lead? What quality does God's way of living exemplify? How is eternity lived and enacted?

There are many ways this question might be answered. But in the context of section 19, I think we get two clear examples of how eternity is enacted, here and now, in mortality. In the first case, the

Lord himself exemplifies how to do eternity. In the second case, the Lord urges Martin Harris, in his own sphere, to live this same way.

In both cases, it seems to me, the quality at stake in eternity is what we might call, taking a little liberty, "vicarity." Am I willing to live and love and sacrifice *on behalf of others*—that is, vicariously—or will I insist on living only on behalf of myself? Will I consecrate my life and property and live as a steward and caretaker?[6] Or will I try to keep my life and property and live as an owner and proprietor?

In the first case, the Lord himself shows us how to sacrifice vicariously, how to live on behalf of others.

"Every man must repent or suffer," the Lord bluntly declares (19:4). Repentance, though, is only possible because God has already acted on our behalf. He's already suffered vicariously. He's already "borne our griefs, and carried our sorrows" (Isaiah 53:4).

"For behold, I, God, have suffered these things for all, that they might not suffer if they would repent; but if they would not repent they must suffer even as I; which suffering caused myself, even God, the greatest of all, to tremble because of pain, and to bleed at every pore, and to suffer both body and spirit—and would that I might not drink the bitter cup, and shrink—nevertheless, glory be to the Father, and I partook and finished my preparations unto the children of men" (19:16–19).

Suffering on our behalf, Christ's life and will are not his own. Acting on our behalf, he acts in the name of the Father. "I am Jesus Christ; I came by the will of the Father, and I do his will" (19:24).

Atonement is one powerful name for how God redeems time and fills it with eternity.

In the second case, the Lord commands Martin to repent and, in Martin's own small way, to do likewise. He commands Martin to open his blind eyes and see how God is already among us. He commands him to consecrate everything and live as God lives.

As section 19 frames it, the *consequence* for not repenting is the terrible (and lonely) burden of unredeemed suffering. "Repent or suffer" (19:4). But the *opposite* of repenting is what the Lord calls "coveting."

To repent is to return to God what he's already claimed as his own—our sorrows and suffering included.

To covet is to treat as our own what belongs to another.

In this case, the Lord tells Martin, "I command thee that thou shalt not covet thy neighbor's wife; nor seek thy neighbor's life" (19:25). This, of course, makes sense because neither the neighbor's wife nor the neighbor's life are Martin's own.

But then the following verse expands the scope of this commandment in a dramatic way: "And again, I command thee that thou shalt not covet thine *own* property, but impart it freely to the printing of the Book of Mormon, which contains the truth and the word of God" (19:26; emphasis added).

Martin is commanded to stop coveting his own property. He's commanded to stop coveting his own life. He's commanded to stop shrinking in fear from the only truth that could ever redeem him, from the mystery of godliness hidden in plain view: that his life wasn't, isn't, and never could be simply his own.

The truth is that, from all eternity to all eternity, Martin's life already belonged to God—and, too, that God's own life was already promised to him.

Coveting—treating as my own what is not my own, my own life included—is, I think, one good name for the blindness at the root of my badness. Coveting paralyzes me with the fear of losing what was not truly my own in the first place. And, thus, coveting condemns me to suffering again what God has already suffered on my behalf.

Coveting, I misunderstand eternity. I misunderstand who God is and what redemption looks like.

Coveting, I commodify eternity and treat as a private quantity what can, in the end, only be enjoyed as a shared quality.

"Pay the debt thou hast contracted with the printer," the Lord commands Martin, and "release thyself from bondage" (19:35).

This is the procedure: stop coveting and be released from bondage.

Adam

Adam,

I've always been struck by the strangeness of the key phrase you identified: "thou shalt not covet thine own property" (19:26). It's strange partly because we simply don't hear the verb *covet* used in that way often. But it's stranger because, once heard, it makes such perfect psychological sense. I recognize, in the instant of hearing the words, exactly what it feels like both to know that I am called to give up something precious *and* to suppress that call covetously. It feels like pulling the blankets over my head, like hiding my candle quietly under a bushel, like stashing my silver under the sofa cushions. I see exactly what you mean: covetousness *is* a kind of blindness, a kind of darkness.

We've promised our readers seven visions of Christ in the pages of this book. Vision requires one key element: light. We'll need a lot of light to deliver on our promise, and we'll need it from all directions—the low-angled seep of sunrise and the noontime flood. We'll need a light "above the brightness of the sun," like the one that fell over a boy prophet more than two hundred years ago (Joseph Smith—History 1:16). Happily, the Doctrine and Covenants is radiant with the presence of Christ. He is the personage we will see in these seven visions, of course, but—more—he is the light that makes all else visible.

Before I start to sketch the vision of Christ that's come into focus for me in Doctrine and Covenants 19, it's worth spending a moment thinking about the particular quality of the light that streams from him over this text. As you say, the Doctrine and Covenants casts a new light on old scripture. And it seems to me that the power of this light to unveil the Restoration's radical reboot of Christianity lies in its strongly directional quality: this is a light that comes *from* somewhere. It's not the diffuse illumination of a tasteful ceiling fixture, much less the flattering glow of a screen-top ring light. No, this is a powerful spotlight on the horizon. It casts long shadows.

The light from Christ cast over this section is, decidedly, an end-time light. It comes from the latter-day shore of God's saving intervention in human history, from the far side of atonement and redemption, of cross and tomb and the Easter sunrise. This is the ascended Lord, and he shines with Monday's sun.

I noticed a profusion of endings right away in this section. "I am Alpha and Omega, . . . the beginning and the end" (19:1). Endings show up throughout the text, but especially at its beginning. Christ has "finished the will of . . . the Father," retaining power to subdue sin and death "at the end of the world, and the last great day of judgment" (19:2–3). He has faithfully borne his sufferings and "finished [his] preparations unto the children of men" (19:19). He is the Messiah "who has already come" (19:27), and this is his "great and the last commandment" to Martin, a divine word which should "suffice . . . even unto the end of [his] life" (19:32).

And, as you've pointed out, the mystery that is clarified for Martin Harris in this section is all about an ending, as well: "it is not written that there shall be no end to this torment" (19:6). There is, already prepared and available to all, an end to the crushing burden of sin. There is "peace in [Christ]" (19:23). In Martin's commandment, the sharply slanted light comes from the postascension Christ, who, situated in the latter phase of salvation history, has himself become the "end of the law" (Romans 10:4)—the culmination or destination, the guiding orientation, of our "daily walk" with God (19:32).

In the apocalyptic end-light of this text, Jesus's life assumes an unexpected shape, like an anamorphic painting that reveals its image only when viewed from the far side. From a blinkered human perspective, standing squarely in front of the canvas, Jesus's life is shaped a bit like a Nike swoosh: it begins from an initial high point during the premortal existence and his premortal ministry, extends through the humility of his mortal birth, and rises in a sustained surge of magnitude and power in his ministry, his mighty atonement, and his final exaltation at the right hand of the Father. Swoosh!

But from the far side of resurrection, in the Christ-light that suffuses Doctrine and Covenants 19, Jesus's life looks different. The end comes at the beginning, as I've noted: Christ is at his mightiest and greatest from the outset of section 19, subduing all things and retaining all power in his identity as "endless" and "eternal" (19:10–12), destroyer of Satan and judge of the world. After that, the section seems, over the course of its instruction to Martin, to register a steady focusing or concentration of Christ's power: not that his power is reduced in any way, but rather Christ's own will is contracted into "the will of the Father" (19:24).

The climax of the section, Christ's own firsthand account of his suffering, coincides with the moment of greatest contraction, marked by that indelible verb "shrink" (19:18). Our modern edition of this revelation follows the word with a cosmos-shattering em dash, in my judgment the most inspired insertion of punctuation in the canon. "That I might not drink the bitter cup, and shrink—" (19:18). What sign could better convey the "groanings which cannot be uttered," the black-hole density of a God's "obedien[ce] unto death" (Romans 8:26; Philippians 2:8)?

After the vision of Christ's passion fades to black, the text resets.

It revisits the call to repentance of the section's opening—"I command you again to repent, lest I humble you with my almighty power," and, yes, "misery thou shalt receive if thou wilt slight these counsels"—but this time with a different mood (19:20, 33). Now the Lord speaks to Martin intimately, invoking Martin's personal experience rather than cosmic cataclysms (see 19:20). He invites Martin to walk in the "meekness" and "peace" of life in Christ (19:23). He speaks now of the good news, the "glad tidings" of the gospel, rather than of the bad news at his left hand (19:29). He instructs Martin to "[revile] not against revilers" (19:30). The mood is one of humility, trust, meekness, and gentleness—Christ's and, in emulation, Martin's. The section ends as it began, with Christ announcing his nearness, but now, instead of Alpha and Omega, the approaching destroyer of evil, we see a beseeching friend: "Yea, come unto me thy Savior" (19:41).

Viewed from the end of the section, from resurrection-side, Christ's life looks like a powerful, controlled decrescendo. There has been no actual diminution of his power or glory or justice. But from the far edge of the canvas, where Christ leads us over the course of this commandment to Martin Harris, that power somehow shows up differently. Why is that? What is it, specifically, about the meaning of the Resurrection that changes the way Christ's power shows up? What is the "mystery of godliness" (19:10) that the slanted end-light of resurrection unlocks?

No doubt there are many ways to answer that question. But here I want to suggest that one answer is *glory*. What is different about the postresurrection, postascension Christ? He was "raised up from the dead by the glory of the Father" (Romans 6:4) and now dwells in "the glory of the Son, on the right hand of the Father" (Doctrine and Covenants 76:20). The postresurrection Christ of Doctrine and Covenants 19 is now, in all respects, *glorious*, having been raised from death and from dust by and in the glory of God. What is *glory*, though?

In the scriptures, *glory* signifies not just generic magnificence but specifically the brilliance and power that emanate from the presence of God. Sometimes the word is used loosely to mean something like "honor" or "high reputation" that is compared or ascribed to God. Under this loose definition, this word, I confess, is one that I sometimes tune out when I read scripture, skipping over it unconsciously as a filler word to make a passage seem grander. But most of the time, when glory gets mentioned, it's as the sign or manifestation of God's essence *being there*. The Bible Dictionary defines *glory* as "some outward and visible manifestation of God's presence."[7] When I try to mentally substitute the word for the more specific meaning—"the sign that God is present in this place"—I've found that a passage can come to life for me.

Not surprisingly, then, *glory* almost always accompanies visions of God in which the divine presence is made visible, typically in dazzling light. The children of Israel, covenanting with God at Sinai, declare that "the Lord our God hath shewed us his glory and his greatness, and we have heard his voice out of the midst of the fire" (Deuteronomy 5:24). Paul's vision of Jesus of Nazareth on the Damascus road leaves him so dazzled that he "could not see for the glory of that light" and had to be led by his friends (Acts 22:11). Of the two personages who stood above him in the air, Joseph Smith says that their "brightness and glory defy all description" (Joseph Smith—History 1:17). We'll see glory show up over and over as we explore these seven visions—and as I suggested above, I think we'll want to attend both to the personage of Christ and to all that is revealed in his light.

So we can say that the kind of light radiated by the end-time Christ of Doctrine and Covenants 19 is, in particular, the glory that attends his dwelling place at the right hand of the Father. The first words of the section—"I am Alpha and Omega, . . . the beginning and the end"—are a scriptural link to the opening of the book of Revelation, where Christ introduces himself in the same terms when John sees him beside the throne of God—which is, yes, extremely glorious (see Revelation 1:8, 13–16). As Alpha and Omega, at the beginning and at the end, Christ has been sustained by God before and during his mortal life. And now, after his passion and ascension, his unity with the Father is completely displayed. He fully manifests divine glory.

And we can say even more about glory because the scriptures pinpoint a particular way in which glory is mirrored between heaven and earth. God is the source, of course, because he is the source of divine presence. But he shares himself with his children in the act of creation, and thus we carry glory within us in the very fact that we have been created. It's a little like this: when I think about myself *as a daughter*, my father and mother automatically become a part of that self because I am a daughter inasmuch as they are my parents. In the same way, my createdness folds the Creator into my being— or, better, the other way round: I am glorious inasmuch as I am his.

That gift of glory, the manifestation of God's brilliant essence in his sons and daughters, happens both at creation and, especially, at new creation, the new life we receive when we are born again in Christ. Paul teaches this, with virtuosic scriptural wordplay, when he writes that "God, who commanded the light to shine out of darkness, hath shined in our hearts, to give the light of the knowledge of the glory of God in the face of Jesus Christ" (2 Corinthians 4:6). God, he's saying, manifests in us his creative presence precisely in the fact of our createdness. And how does it show up? As "the glory of God in the face of Jesus Christ."

And then comes the crucial final step: we mirror our created glory back to God in the form of praise, which is nothing more than a grateful acknowledgement of the Creator. You see this all over the scriptures when you start looking for it. Anytime you see a variation of the formula "Glory be to God," the speaker is reflecting back to God the divine light that she bears in the fact of her createdness. The technical term for this type of prayer is *doxology*, a delicious word in itself, but the point is that this form of praise is not just a general hyping up of God as amazing and powerful. By invoking glory, doxology specifically (1) acknowledges our createdness, which is to say the foundation of our being in relationship to God; (2) names the divine presence we ourselves manifest at new creation; and (3) praises God as the creator of new light. A clear example is Romans 11:36, where Paul confesses that "of him, and through him, and to him, are all things: to whom be glory for ever." Glory with the Father and the Son, the end we hope for, continually takes us back to the beginning.

In this gift of glory that is given to us (as the radiance of divine light) by the Creator through creation and our return of this gift (as praise), we start to understand the special trick of light in Doctrine and Covenants 19 that shows us Christ's life as a great decrescendo. The conventional meaning of *glory* has been turned inside out: rather than signifying honor and acclaim for my own achievement, it now signifies, on the contrary, a debt to God at the foundation of my life. As King Benjamin puts it, "In the first place, he hath created you, and granted unto you your lives, for which ye are indebted unto him" (Mosiah 2:23). And because my createdness by another is a reality that can never be expunged from that "first place," even "if [I] should render all the thanks and praise which [my] whole soul has power to possess, to that God who has created [me], . . . yet [I] would be unprofitable" (Mosiah 2:20–21). This is glory?! Yes, I think so. This is God's glory. Glory be to God.

And this, I suggest, is just what we see happening in Doctrine and Covenants 19. While the word *glory* isn't splashed all over the section, it shows up in several crucial spots. Just at the fine point of

Christ's decrescendo, right after that earth-shattering dash, he says: "Nevertheless, glory be to the Father, and I partook and finished my preparations unto the children of men" (19:19). Did you catch that doxology? "Glory be to the Father." Christ himself was the Father's agent of creation in the beginning, of course, but here, in the middle of the middle of time, he acts in full solidarity with humankind's creatureliness, giving back to God as praise the radiance that God has instilled in his beloved son.

By uttering this prayer at the moment of greatest temptation, on the point of shrinking away from the pain and suffering of his bitter cup, he teaches a great sermon on the paradox of glory: the strength to bear up—to partake and finish what life asks of us—comes not from our inner riches but from our inner indebtedness, not from our personal greatness but from our creaturely dependence. It's only when the Savior names his dependence on the Father by returning glory in prayer that he gathers the strength to drink to the dregs. And now that we recognize it, we can see that this paradox has been in effect from the very beginning of the section, when Christ announces that he, "having accomplished and finished the will of him whose I am, even the Father," has done so "that I might subdue all things unto myself" (19:2). Christ's heroic feat of will, the subduction of death and sin, is qualified with the acknowledgement that he belongs to the Father and that his will is not his own. This is glory?! This is glory.

The paradox of glory helps explain the curious ambiguity in the word *shrink,* the most memorable image, I think, in this vision of Christ. Given the grammar and punctuation of verse 18, it's difficult to tell whether Christ is tempted to shrink or not to shrink. Is the Savior tempted to "shrink away" from the suffering, or is he tempted *not* to "shrink" his own will?

His suffering, he says, caused him "to suffer both body and spirit—and would that I might not drink the bitter cup, and shrink."

In this sentence of many clauses, does "and shrink" stand independently from "not drink the bitter cup" as something that his weak flesh wants, something that he is tempted to do? Is he saying, in effect, (1) "I wished *to not drink* the bitter cup, and (2) I wished *to shrink*"? In this reading, Christ's shrinking is the opposite of drinking the bitter cup; it refers to his innate human desire to "shrink away" from pain and suffering. This is perhaps the more common interpretation of this verse.

But there's another possible interpretation. Is "shrink" here bundled with "drink the bitter cup" as something that Christ is tempted *not* to do? Is he saying, "I wished (1) that I would *not have to drink* the bitter cup and (2) that I would *not have to shrink*." If this is the proper parsing of the grammar, it seems shrinking is *equivalent* to drinking the bitter cup, not its opposite. It is a shrinking of his own will, his own human instinct for self-preservation. This is a less familiar interpretation, but I find its implications compelling.

That ambiguity, together with the powerful sense of identification it generates in readers, is what makes this passage electric. I know immediately and instinctively both of these shrinkings. I have been tempted many times to shrink away from the bitter cup served me; conversely, I often allow my own will to balloon in panic and shame rather than contract in love. I don't think we can fully determine the significance of the word *shrink*—whether a powerful contraction of the Savior's will in submission to the Father, or a fearful recoil from the suffering he faces—in the text we have, and I think that's okay. The paradox of glory makes sense of both readings simultaneously. Christ's glory is a victory of submission: a shrinking *of* his own will in acknowledgement of his creaturely dependence so that he might not shrink *from* the work that is his.

It's this affirmative sense of *shrink*—shrinking as the loving contraction of the will—that I think the Savior wants us to see when he shines the slanting light of his exalted glory over the events of the Atonement and thereby transforms the shape of his life. When the text resets in the middle and then repeats the call to repentance in a contracted mode, it doesn't so much explain the paradox of glory as enact it before our reading eyes. It wants to call our hearts more than inform our minds. As Christ himself puts it, section 19 "is more express than other scriptures, that it might work upon the hearts of the children of men, altogether for my name's glory" (19:7).

The scriptures, if we let them work upon our hearts, can be the site where God's presence in the world is manifest as glory, the brilliant light of new creation. Glory be to God.

Rosalynde

— CHAPTER 2 —

The Christ Who Comes

DOCTRINE AND COVENANTS 45

In this revelation, Christ speaks as Creator, Advocate, and Savior; he is Alpha and Omega, the light shining in the darkness. He describes the future scene of his second coming amid the clouds of heaven, clothed in glory, when he will show his wounds to his people. He teaches that the righteous city of Enoch was reserved in Christ and is promised to all holy people. Christ revealed the signs of his coming to his disciples on the Mount of Olives. The fulness of the gospel will be restored as the sign of the fig tree's leaf; some will reject it. The wise who have received both the truth and the Spirit will abide the Lord's coming, and the Lord will be in their midst as king and lawgiver.

Joseph Smith is commanded to begin the translation of the New Testament. The Saints are commanded to gather, contribute their resources, and purchase lands for the New Jerusalem, a place of peace, refuge, and safety. The glory of the Lord will be there, and the peaceful people of every nation will flock to it with songs of joy.

> "And they shall see me in the clouds of heaven, clothed with power and great glory." (Doctrine and Covenants 45:44)

Rosalynde,

You're right that it's easy to forget about the light. It's easy to see what there is to see but then miss the light that makes everything visible in the first place.

"Glory," as you suggest, is a good name for Christ's light. It's a good name for God's manifest presence.

This light, as we'll soon see, is literally "the light of the sun, and the power thereof by which it was made," even as it is also "the same light that quickeneth [our] understandings; which light proceedeth forth from the presence of God to fill the immensity of space" (Doctrine and Covenants 88:7, 11–12).

The fact that this light is *everywhere*—literally "in all things" (Doctrine and Covenants 88:13)—is, I think, part of what makes it so hard to see. This light is so obvious and so familiar as to be invisible. We take it for granted. We look past it—or, better, *through* it—because, to make everything else visible, the light itself must be clear like a windowpane.

And I appreciate, too, your reading of Doctrine and Covenants 19:18's pivotal word, *shrink*. "Which suffering caused myself, even God, the greatest of all, to tremble because of pain" and "would that I might not drink the bitter cup, and shrink."

There is always the temptation to shrink from difficulty and sacrifice. But there is also always the temptation to *not* shrink— the temptation to make myself bigger, to puff myself up and, thus, block God's light. For God's light to shine in me and through me, I must get out of the way. My own will, like Christ's, must become translucent.

This, as the Lord describes it in section 45, is the continual danger: that God's light will break forth but no one will *see* it. "A light shall break forth among them that sit in darkness," but those sitting in darkness "receive it not; for they perceive not the light" (45:28, 29).

Or, as the Lord says in verse 7, recasting John 1:5, "I am Alpha and Omega, . . . a light that shineth in darkness and the darkness comprehendeth it not."

To avoid this blindness and escape this darkness, I must learn how to "perceive" this light. I must learn how to "comprehend" it.

This is the disciple's task: to watch for the breaking of this divine light.

And this is the burden of section 45, to help prepare the Church as a whole for the "breaking forth" of this light at Christ's second coming.

Section 45 comes as a revelation through Joseph Smith to the Church in March 1831. In terms of practical instructions, the revelation has two takeaways.

First, the Lord commands the Saints to "gather up your riches that ye may purchase an inheritance"—that is, "a land of peace, a city of refuge, a place of safety" where a New Jerusalem can be built (45:65, 66). And second, the Lord gives Joseph Smith permission to move on from translating the Old Testament and begin working on an inspired version of the New Testament. "I give unto you that ye may now translate it," the Lord says of the New Testament, "that ye may be prepared for the things to come" (45:61). This work of translating the New Testament is meant, quite specifically, to prepare both the Prophet and the Saints for the world's end.

These practical instructions, though, take only a handful of the section's seventy-five verses.

What's going on in all those other verses?

The rest of the section unfolds as the Lord's own extended commentary on his apocalyptic discourse originally given in Matthew 24. And this fresh retelling of Matthew 24's vision of the world's end sets a dramatic stage for the practical instructions that close out the revelation. On one hand, this retelling of Matthew 24 explains why the Saints need to quickly gather money, buy land, and start building a refuge in Zion: because great tribulations are coming and the world's end is near. And on the other hand, this retelling both models and authorizes Joseph Smith's own expansive and inspired translation of the New Testament text. In this sense, section 45 is a kind of case study, volunteered by Christ himself, that exemplifies how to give inspired amplifications of canonical texts.

The visionary centerpiece of both Matthew 24 and Doctrine and Covenants 45 is quite familiar and has been depicted in paintings and stained-glass windows for thousands of years, with reproductions of Harry Anderson's own rendition often commanding pride of place in the lobbies of our chapels.

As originally given by Jesus in Matthew 24:30–31, the central image is as follows: "And then shall appear the sign of the Son of man in heaven: and then shall all the tribes of the earth mourn, and they shall see the Son of man coming in the clouds of heaven with power and great glory. And he shall send his angels with a great sound of a trumpet, and they shall gather together his elect from the four winds, from one end of heaven to the other."

This image is repeated twice in the text of Doctrine and Covenants 45.

The image is anticipated in verse 16 when Christ prefaces his retelling of Matthew 24 by reminding us how he once spoke to his own disciples, saying: "Ye have asked of me concerning the signs of my coming, in the day when I shall come in my glory in the clouds of heaven, to fulfil the promises that I have made unto your fathers."

And the image is retrieved in full, at the heart of Matthew 24's retelling, in verses 44 and 45: "And then they shall look for me, and, behold, I will come; and they shall see me in the clouds of heaven, clothed with power and great glory; with all the holy angels; and he that watches not for me shall be cut off. But before the arm of the Lord shall fall, an angel shall sound his trump, and the saints that have slept shall come forth to meet me in the cloud."

This is the vision: Christ, clothed with power and great glory, coming in the clouds of heaven.

For my part, though, this image doesn't prompt me to picture something like Anderson's towering, sky-blue painting. Rather, my mind goes straight to a small, 3×5, black-and-white photograph of Jesus taped into the back of my battered mission scriptures.

If the prospect of such a photograph sounds strange to you, you'd be right. It is.

How, you might ask, did I come by a photo of Jesus?

I served my mission in New Mexico. I spent most of my time either in Albuquerque or up in the "Four Corners," where the right-angled borders of New Mexico, Arizona, Colorado, and Utah all converge in a neat grid. One of my areas in the Four Corners was bisected by a river. On the far side of the river, our area extended out into the desert, onto Navajo land. On the near side of the river, a whole community (originally a Latter-day Saint colony) was tucked into a tree-lined valley that tracked the river's path. In this valley lived a woman who became a dear friend.

Everyone just called her "Grandma," and we did the same. I'm guessing she must have been at least eighty. Her glasses were wide and thick. Her eyesight poor. Her hair permed. Her back stooped. Her frame slender. But her hands were strong and her testimony of the Restoration unshakable.

Missionaries had been visiting her since time immemorial. Situated at a crossroads, her small house was a convenient place to stop for a glass of water or, simply, to sit for a few minutes in that slack hour between knocking on doors and dinner. She was always home. She always welcomed us. She always had an encouraging word to say. And though her eyes were weak, she was a keen observer of people. She had no illusions about any of us, and still, she loved all of us—it didn't matter whether we were "good" missionaries, "bad" missionaries, or hardly missionaries at all.

I spent a long time in her area, outlasting several companions. We became close.

I don't remember what originally prompted her to share the photo. But one day, late in my tenure, she said she had something she wanted to show me. She shuffled back into her bedroom, riffled through some papers, and came back with a yellowed photo in hand. She eased back into her chair, then leaned forward, elbows on her knees, and handed it to me.

It was a black-and-white photo of an afternoon sky.

The gray sky was full of puffy white clouds. The sun, slanted.

And there, among those rolling clouds, clearly floated the image of a tiny man, serene, arms outstretched—distant, yes, but clothed in something like a robe, his face too blurry to show any features beyond a beard.

I looked at that photo for a long time. I didn't know what to think.

She said she hadn't taken the photo herself. But she claimed to have some connection to the man who did. One afternoon, she said, he'd felt compelled to put down what he was doing, get his camera, and snap a picture of the afternoon sky. He didn't know why. But he did it. He looked up, pointed his camera into the void, clicked the shutter, and then went back to work. Only later, she said, after he developed the film, did he find anything more than just clouds.

I don't know if this story is true. She believed it was.

I don't have the original photo, but she let me make a copy that, to this day, is taped into the back of my scriptures.

Do I think this man actually captured a snapshot of Jesus in the sky? To me, that seems surpassingly improbable.

Why, then, did I keep it? And why am I telling you about it?

Because I love Grandma.

I love that she loved this photo. And I love that she lived in a world of faith, watchful and attentive and expectant, where such a photo was entirely plausible.

Skeptical as I tend to be, I don't want to live in a world where her faith—her solid, tangible, documentable faith—doesn't manifest its own real-world mass and force. She didn't have faith because of that photo. It was, at best, a curiosity to her. A hint. But I think, like me, she was interested in that photo because she *already* had faith. She was interested in that photo because she'd already dedicated her whole life to doing what Jesus had asked: she'd spent her life *watching* for him to come. She'd kept her eyes open to his light when, all around her, people were busy and blind, unable to see the light as it broke forth. And for this same reason, I think, she was also always able to see Christ's blurry image in *us*, in the hundreds of implausible missionaries who passed through her living room over the years, all of us just hoping for a glass of water, a place to sit, and someone willing to welcome us as we were.

Committed to watching for his coming, she learned how to see him everywhere she looked.

This, though, is not an easy thing to do. It requires patience and discipline. It requires sacrifice and consecration. And, especially, it requires a willingness to live with our eyes wide open to the fact that the world is going to end.

"Ye say that ye know that the end of the world cometh; ye say also that ye know that the heavens and the earth shall pass away" (45:22)—but do we really? Have you and I really looked this most basic truth square in the eye? And do we go beyond just acknowledging it—grudgingly, abstractly, theoretically—to spend, instead, our days *watching* for it?

"Then they shall look for me, and, behold, I will come," and "he that watches not for me shall be cut off" (45:44).

It's true that people have been watching for Christ's return for thousands of years, and even now, we're still waiting, still watching, still doing the same. But this delay doesn't undercut the value of all that watching because, regardless of whether the end has arrived for the whole world, that same end is coming swiftly and inescapably for *me*. And, as a result, that same watchful posture is just as necessary.

And this, in fact, is how the entirety of section 45's meditation on the apocalypse begins, with an exhortation to wake up to my own mortality: "Hearken, O ye people of my church. . . . Hearken unto my voice, lest death shall overtake you; in an hour when ye think not the summer shall be past, and the harvest ended" (45:1–2).

Grandma has long since been overtaken by death. But I'd wager any sum that she wasn't surprised. Given her willingness to watch for Christ, her end was no thief in the night.

She already knew that we are only "strangers and pilgrims on the earth" (45:13). And because she was willing to "behold the sufferings and death of him who did no sin," she was also able to see this "light that shineth in darkness" (45:4, 7).

She recognized Christ not only as her Alpha but also as her Omega. "I am Alpha *and* Omega," Christ says, "the beginning *and* the end" (45:7; emphasis added).

To believe in Christ is to believe in both. It's to watch and pray for both. To believe in Christ is to endure not just *to* the end but straight *through* that end to the new worlds that inevitably follow.

May we all endure through the end!

Godspeed, Grandma.

Adam

> "With him that cometh I will reason as with men in days of old, and I will show unto you my strong reasoning. Wherefore, hearken ye together and let me show unto you even my wisdom." (Doctrine and Covenants 45:10–11)

Adam,

I think I'll see Grandma's snapshot in my mind right beside Harry Anderson's trumpeting angels whenever I think of the Second Coming. Those juxtaposed images—one iconic, triumphal; the other personal, enigmatic—remind me of what President Jeffery R. Holland once said in a large room where we sat together in the audience: "Regarding what the scriptures call 'the day of [the] Lord Jesus Christ' [1 Corinthians 1:8], I imagine not only the dramatic, universal appearance of His light coming out of the East and His descent upon the two Jerusalems, but I imagine also a more personal encounter—a solitary Christ standing at a solitary door, knocking."[8]

Grandma's snapshot, despite the clouds and the million-mile sky, feels to me like that "more personal encounter." And I can imagine just what it must have felt like to spend an hour in Grandma's house, refuge from the afternoon sun, and rest in her unconditional welcome. It must have felt like a blessing.

I had a place like that on my mission. My first summer in the Portuguese interior occasionally reached 40 degrees Celsius, the dreaded "quarenta graus" (that's 104 degrees Fahrenheit). My companion and I were always on foot, weary and hot. One day we spotted an enormous fig tree just off the path between our apartment and the storefront meetinghouse. Its branches bowed nearly to the ground, and we found that we could push through them into the tree's interior, a shaded green room tall enough to stand upright. Ripe figs hung all around us, their sweet pink flesh a surprise I don't think I'll ever get over. We rested and feasted, and even the memory makes me want to praise God for those moments of relief.

Grandma is gone. Chances are the fig tree has fallen to an apartment *bloco*, though I've never been back to see. All things come to an end. And I suppose that's where section 45 comes in.

This revelation gives us not only the indelible image of Christ's second coming; it gives us a whole montage of Christ's mortal and postmortal ministry. We're shown scenes of Christ advocating before the Father (see 45:3–5), preaching to his disciples on the Mount of Olives (see 45:16), ministering tenderly to the Jewish remnant after his return (see 45:51–52), and standing in Zion's midst as lawgiver and king (see 45:59).

I think we can use these vividly rendered scenes as guideposts to the hidden structure of this long revelation. Over the course of seventy-five verses, Christ calls to his people in three voices. First, he calls them as their Creator, and he gives that call a visual punch with a brief but action-packed cosmic scene: "Give ear to him who laid the foundation of the earth, who made the heavens and all the hosts thereof, and by whom all things were made which live, and move, and have a being" (45:1). We see his mighty hands opening space between heaven and earth and filling that world with living breath.

Next, Christ calls his people as their Savior: "Hearken unto my voice, lest death shall overtake you; in an hour when ye think not the summer shall be past, and the harvest ended, and your souls not saved" (45:2). He illustrates this call with another visual scene, this time showing his sacrifice for the human family: "behold the blood of thy Son which was shed, the blood of him whom thou gavest that thyself might be glorified" (45:4). In the lifeblood he twice evokes,

I see the suffering God of section 19, weeping red at every pore (see 19:18).

Finally, Christ calls his people in the voice of their Teacher: "Hearken ye together and let me show unto you even my wisdom" (45:11). It's in this voice—the patient, reasonable voice of a learned rabbi imparting hidden wisdom—that Christ offers a visual scene of his role as Teacher, as he did in the voices of Creator and Savior. We are shown Christ with his disciples sitting atop the Mount of Olives. As you pointed out, Adam, Christ is here recreating and interpreting for modern readers the text of Matthew 24 and 25, his prophecy of God's work as it will unfold in the latter days.

This scene turns out to be long and rather complex, including several nested scenes-within-the-scene, as he gives to his New Testament disciples precisely what he's giving in section 45: a revelation packed with memorable visual images that speak to the imagination and emotion—the kind of "express" teaching that "work[s] upon the hearts of the children of men," as we learned in Doctrine and Covenants 19:7.

As Teacher, Christ first gives an outline of how God will shape history after his death and resurrection: from the near-term destruction of the Jerusalem temple, definitively ending the old covenant, through the scattering of Israel and the calamitous "times of the Gentiles" (45:25–30), and finally to the appearance of the brilliant light of the Restoration, the gathering up of the remnant of Israel and the just from all nations, and the coming of Christ in glory to the earth. Christ concludes his survey of salvation history with a glimpse of his millennial reign in the Zion community of those who have seen his light. Section 45 surveys God's determination to "bring to pass the immortality and eternal life of man" (Moses 1:39) and strings it on the wire of human history at an epic scale.

I imagine the Teacher seated in the sloping duff of the Mount of Olives. There he delivers three secrets nested within this outline of sacred history, and once again he illustrates each with a memorable visual image. First, pairing in verse 17 the predicaments of the scattered house of Israel and the deceased souls who "have looked upon the long absence of [their] spirits from [their] bodies to be a bondage," Christ teaches that we "gather the elect of the Lord on both sides of the veil," as President Russell M. Nelson has taught.[9]

This lesson is illustrated with what to me is the most poignant visual of section 45: the picture of Christ standing among the remnant of Israel, those who have seen the latter-day light break and followed it faithfully into the presence of Christ. Christ ministers to this greening remnant just as he did in his postresurrection ministries in Jerusalem and Bountiful: he displays the wounds in his hands and his feet, prints that visibly testify of his identity. "These wounds are the wounds with which I was wounded in the house of my friends. I am he who was lifted up. I am Jesus that was crucified. I am the Son of God" (45:52; see also Zechariah 12–13). The weeping of the remnant in that moment shows me that mourning is folded into the joy of deliverance.

Next, Christ gives his disciples a reading lesson. The latter-day events he describes are not points on a timeline; they are signs. As signs, they must be read rightly to decode their meaning. He teaches his disciples to read in this way with, as we've come to expect, a visual image: "Ye look and behold the fig trees, and ye see them with your eyes, and ye say when they begin to shoot forth, and their leaves are yet tender, that summer is now nigh at hand; even so it shall be in that day when they shall see all these things, then shall they know that the hour is nigh" (45:37–38).

To read the sign of the fig tree, you must first watch for it. The most important thing I do for my backyard garden each day is simply to look at it carefully: Is anybody wilting? Is there evidence of pest damage? Who is setting fruit? Who needs to be pruned? We often read latter-day signs of the times as warnings that the world will end—and "in this ye say truly, for so it is" (45:23). But isn't the green sign of the fig tree also just the opposite? Fig leaves unfurl in late spring. Their appearance signals that a new season is beginning. Christ is Alpha and Omega, beginning and end; the "summer [is] past" (45:2), and the "summer is now nigh at hand" (45:37). As you put it, Adam, "To believe in Christ is to endure not just to the end but straight through that end to the new worlds that inevitably follow." The signs of the latter days are a message that the new world has been inaugurated.

The form and place of that inauguration is the Master's final secret. Recall that his first words in the voice of the Teacher spoke of the wisdom of "the God of Enoch, and his [people]" (45:11), that band of believers whose holy city God took to his bosom. Ever since that time, pilgrims have searched for that city, where they will no longer be strangers but friends—and the Teacher now promises "that they should find it and see it in their flesh" (45:14). The conclusion of the long scene on the Mount of Olives, and the remainder of section 45, concern this latter-day city of Zion. Christ summons the image of a wedding feast to teach the disciples where to find the city—he doesn't paint much of a word picture this time but just drops a reference to the parable of the ten virgins (see 45:56).

Perhaps it was getting uncomfortable on the rocky slope and the Teacher knew it was time to wrap up the lesson. Still, a brief reference is all it takes to evoke the anticipation of the bridegroom's chamber, the dark boredom of the passing hours, and the sudden gleam of lamplight. And the point is clear: the bridegroom's chamber is the holy city, and pilgrims who watch for the sign of the fig tree will be guided there by the Holy Spirit. At midnight, the chamber will fill with light and song, and "the Lord shall be in their midst, and his glory shall be upon them, and he will be their king and their lawgiver" (45:59).

Step back to look at the images of Christ given in their entirety for a moment: the cosmic builder of earth and heaven, the suffering Savior at the throne of God, the Rabbi of ancient wisdom on the Mount of Olives, the resurrected Lord among the weeping remnant of Israel, the festal Bridegroom come to dwell in the midst of his people.

Of all these images, it's the one most sparsely rendered—Christ as Bridegroom, barely sketched in the allusion to the ten virgins— that strikes me on this reading. It teaches something about both the character of Zion and the Christ of the Doctrine and Covenants, and it does so by way of an implicit contrast that's easily missed. Remember how the parable of the ten virgins ends in Matthew 25? The bridegroom finally arrives at midnight, just as the unprepared women have left to purchase more oil. Meanwhile, "they that were ready went in with him to the marriage: and the door was shut" (Matthew 25:10). When the others return, the chamber door is not opened to them. The boundary is unbreachable. The unprepared are locked out.

Now compare Matthew's version of the parable with Doctrine and Covenants 45. Over the course of the revelation, as we've seen, the Lord carefully piques our interest and lays the historical and theological foundation for his culminating teachings about the latter-day city of Zion. As he outlines the calamitous happenings of the "times of the Gentiles" (45:25–30), he reassures his disciples that there is safety for those who embrace the light: they shall "abide the day," and they will "stand in holy places, and shall not be moved" (45:57, 32). Zion will be a "land of peace, a city of refuge, a place of safety" (45:66). Given the earlier allusion to the parable of the ten virgins, it might be reasonable to assume that Zion will be made safe by an unbreachable boundary, like the door of the bridegroom's chamber. Zion will be a fortress for the righteous because it locks the wicked out.

Not so! In contrast to the bridegroom's chamber, the Lord describes latter-day Zion as a city of unlocked doors. The peace lovers of every nation will flock to Zion with joyful songs (see 45:69, 71). But what will keep the warmongers and their bloody swords out? Their own faint hearts and their own faulty assumptions about "glory" and "terror." "The glory of the Lord shall be [in Zion], and the terror of the Lord also shall be there, insomuch that the wicked will not come unto it" (45:67). From the perspective of sin, the brilliant light of the Lord's love provokes dread and avoidance, and thus "it shall be said among the wicked: Let us not go up to battle against Zion, for the inhabitants of Zion are terrible; wherefore we cannot stand" (45:70). In Christ's latter-day telling, there's no need to make of Zion a defensive fortress, no need to lock the place up at midnight, because the warmongers turn themselves away. Zion's door swings freely on its hinges.

And here I'll make a final interpretive step. There's something about the unlocked doors of Zion, its defenseless breachability, that reminds me of the bleeding body of Christ as he's shown it in sections 19 and 45. "Behold the blood of thy Son which was shed," he tells his Father (45:4). He describes the sufferings that caused him "to tremble because of pain, and to bleed at every pore" (19:18). I'm moved by the porousness of Christ's flesh in these scenes, the free passage of blood across the boundary of his body. It's a porousness that leaves him vulnerable to loss and injury yet underscores his love and trust. And the porousness of his body—a defenselessness that all human bodies share—is matched by the openness of his spirit, his desire to be "in my Father, and ye in me, and I in you" (John 14:20). The picture of Zion that concludes section 45, the unlocked fortress secured only by the glory of God shining in its midst, shows us a celebration of such Christlike openness as a joyful counterpoint to earlier scenes of his suffering.

Rosalynde

CHAPTER 3

Christ in the Bosom of the Father

DOCTRINE AND COVENANTS 76

Sidney Rigdon and Joseph Smith, while translating John 5:29, meditate in the Spirit on the Resurrection, and the eyes of their understanding are opened. They see in vision the throne of God and Christ at the right hand of the Father, they see Lucifer's rebellion and fall, and they see the sons of perdition. They understand the glad tidings of the gospel: all other children of God may be saved in Christ.

Sidney and Joseph see the righteous who are raised in the First Resurrection and their exaltation in the celestial world. These are they who see as they are seen, and know as they are known, having received of the Lord's fulness and grace. Joseph and Sidney see the glory of the terrestrial and telestial worlds and their inhabitants, who receive the glory of Christ but not his fulness. Through the Spirit, those who love God and purify themselves may see and know for themselves.

> **"His purposes fail not, neither are there any who can stay his hand." (Doctrine and Covenants 76:3)**

Rosalynde,

I love the idea of you and your companion taking shelter from the Portuguese sun in the shade of an actual fig tree, breathing literal life into Jesus's apocalyptic image—and, unlike Jesus, finding actual figs there, ready to eat! A fig tree to be blessed rather than cursed.

And I especially love what you've done with the image of the bridegroom's chamber from the parable of the ten virgins, observing how section 45 juxtaposes that familiar story about a door being "shut" (Matthew 25:10) with, on the other hand, the promise of Zion, an impregnable fortress whose gates are all unlocked and whose doors are all wide open. "What will keep the warmongers and their bloody swords out?" you ask. "Their own faint hearts and their own faulty assumptions about 'glory' and 'terror'" (see Doctrine and Covenants 45:67).

What could be more terrifying than Zion's wide-open doors? Than God's wide-open arms?

In section 76, those unlocked gates and wide-open doors are the very subject that now takes center stage. Rather than being subtext, they become the substance of the text.

Sketching the whole plan of salvation, section 76 introduces one of the Restoration's most important and surprising doctrines: that there are actually three degrees of postmortal glory and that, as Joseph Smith described it, "the term 'Heaven,' as intended for the Saints' eternal home, must include more kingdoms than one."[10]

This section offers, I think, a strikingly original vision of our possible postmortal lives, a colorful spectrum that rewrites the black-and-white, all-or-nothing stories about heaven and hell we've inherited. And in the process, it clarifies both the nature of God's love and the character of our own promised salvation.

Before looking at the vision itself, I want to reflect for a moment on the circumstances that occasioned it. This, really, is one of my favorite things about the Doctrine and Covenants. We don't simply have these revelations in their final, finished form. We also often get to peek behind the curtain to see *how* these mysteries were revealed. We get to witness the visionary experience itself. And, as a result, these sections frequently reveal—almost like bonus content— important truths about the revelatory process itself.

In this case, the vision opened "on the sixteenth day of February, in the year of our Lord one thousand eight hundred and thirty-two" (76:11). Joseph Smith and Sidney Rigdon were working together on an inspired translation of the New Testament, as previously authorized in section 45. Specifically, they were working on John 5:29.

John 5:29 is about "the resurrection of the dead," and an inspired edit of the passage was given to Joseph and Sidney as follows: and they "shall come forth; they who have done good, in the resurrection of the just; and they who have done evil, in the resurrection of the unjust" (76:16, 17).

This amended translation is, all by itself, a kind of revelation because the King James Version of John 5:29, rather than dividing resurrection into "the just" and "the unjust," contrasts "the resurrection *of life*" with "the resurrection *of damnation*" (emphasis added).

What difference does this edit make?

We might, at least, note that this inspired edit drops any use of the word "damnation," a change in vocabulary that's in keeping with the spirit of section 76's much more expansive view of heaven and salvation. And, what's more, it substitutes for "life" and "damnation" talk about "the just" and "the unjust," categories that we'll soon see are better suited for marking gradations *internal* to heaven's tripartite structure of redemption, instead of a zero-sum distinction between heaven and hell.

Joseph and Sidney report that this inspired edit caused them "to marvel" (76:18). Something previously obscure became, then, perfectly obvious to them both. As the heading to section 76 recounts: "It was apparent that many important points touching the salvation of man had been taken from the Bible, or lost before it was compiled," and thus, "it appeared self-evident from what truths were left" that there must be more than one heavenly kingdom.

This potent combination of "marveling" and "self-evidence" appears to be what occasioned the vision that follows.

"While we meditated upon these things"—meditation being, I think, an apt term for the focused state of mind that follows being struck with wonder by a newly self-evident truth—"the Lord touched the eyes of our understandings and they were opened, and the glory of the Lord shone round about" (76:19).

Allowing for how these different elements would likely bleed into each other in the experience itself, we might still mark the following sequence as preparatory to Joseph and Sidney's visionary experience: (1) a deep and sustained immersion in scripture, (2) an inspired insight that clarifies the meaning of a puzzling passage, (3) marveling at this insight, (4) the lightning bolt of a newly and globally self-evident truth, (5) the onset of a meditative absorption, and *then* finally (6) the opening of a panoramic vision saturated with glory.

Other revelations sketch other possible paths, but something like the above captures crucial elements of how Joseph and Sidney received this particular revelation. And in this sequence of elements, it's especially interesting how the "self-evident" truth of multiple heavenly kingdoms came before, rather than after, the vision. Their *reasoned* discovery of this self-evident idea is what occasioned a full *visionary* experience of the truth.

As the Lord promises in section 45: "With him that cometh I will reason as with men in days of old, and I will show unto you my strong reasoning" (45:10).

Strong reasoning indeed!

But what about the vision itself? What do Joseph and Sidney actually see?

First and foremost, they see Jesus Christ. They see Christ triumphant, seated on a throne. They see the Son reigning at the right hand of the Father.

In general, this first vision follows the familiar pattern set by other throne theophanies: "We beheld the glory of the Son, on the right hand of the Father, and received of his fulness; and saw the holy angels, and them who are sanctified before his throne, worshiping God, and the Lamb" (76:20–21).

This vision of Christ then causes Joseph and Sidney to memorably exclaim: "And now, after the many testimonies which have been given of him, this is the testimony, last of all, which we give of him: That he lives! For we saw him, even on the right hand of God; and we heard the voice bearing record that he is the Only Begotten of the Father—that by him, and through him, and of him, the worlds are and were created, and the inhabitants thereof are begotten sons and daughters unto God" (76:22–24).

This vision of a victorious Christ, triumphant, enthroned at God's right hand, is the essential backdrop for the visions that follow. And, in my view, it's crucial to pair all of the visions that follow in section 76 with this opening vision of unqualified triumph because, ultimately, the question that animates the revelation as a whole is exactly that: what, really, does it *mean* for Christ to be triumphant?

What does it mean to claim that Christ's "purposes fail not" or that "neither are there any who can stay his hand" (76:3)?

In short: what does it mean, ultimately, to say that Christ is going to *win*?

The broader Christian tradition has always acknowledged that Christ will triumph. Christ will win. But section 76, I think, departs sharply from the consensus view, historically, of what this triumph means.

Broadly speaking, I think it's fair to say that the dominant view of Christ's final triumph has traditionally involved (1) Christ saving a small number of the faithful in heaven and (2) Christ damning the vast majority of humanity to hell. On this model, Christ's ultimate triumph consists primarily of defeating those who are evil and punishing them—for all eternity—with the evil they deserve.

In short, victory looks like Christ shutting heaven's doors behind a faithful few, locking up the remainder in hell, and throwing away all the keys, forever. Mission accomplished. The end.

Section 76 turns this old vision of triumph inside out. It refuses to believe that damning most people to hell counts as "winning."

To triumph, Christ doesn't need to *defeat* his enemies. In fact, just the opposite. In order for his divine "purposes [to] fail not," Christ needs his enemies to surrender their weapons, give up being his enemies, and join him. To triumph, Christ must *save* his enemies.

And he saves these enemies by—surprise!—stubbornly loving them, regardless of what it costs him, even if he must then accomplish a "perfect atonement through the shedding of his own blood" (76:69).

These are Zion's marching orders: "Love your enemies, bless them that curse you, do good to them that hate you, and pray for them which despitefully use you, and persecute you" (Matthew 5:44). "For if," as Paul says, "when we were enemies, we were reconciled to God by the death of his Son, much more, being reconciled, we shall be saved by his life" (Romans 5:10).

And these, of course, turn out to be the exact marching orders that (ironically) cause Christ's "enemies" to quake, to tremble, and to shout in fear as they run away: "the inhabitants of Zion are terrible" (Doctrine and Covenants 45:70)!

Perfect love casts out all fear (see 1 John 4:18). But deep-rooted fears run from the vulnerability required for love.

One immediate consequence of this new definition of victory is that section 76 effectively consigns traditional ideas about hell and damnation to the dustbins of history.

It's true that "liars, and sorcerers, and adulterers, and whoremongers, and whosoever loves and makes a lie" may, for a time, be "cast down to hell and suffer the wrath of Almighty God"—but only *until* the fulness of times" when they, too, shall be rescued from this needed purgatory to inherit a kingdom of glory (76:103, 106, emphasis added).

For mortals like us, eternal damnation—that is, damnation without the hope of finding any kingdom of glory—applies only to a vanishingly small number of "sons of perdition" who refuse to be saved in any way, under any circumstances, "having denied the Only Begotten Son of the Father, having crucified him unto themselves and put him to an open shame" (76:32, 35).

These few lonely rebels, section 76 repeatedly insists, are "the only ones who shall not be redeemed in the due time of the Lord" (76:38).

"*All* the rest shall be brought forth by the resurrection of the dead, through the triumph and the glory of the Lamb" (76:39; emphasis added). Why? Because Jesus was "crucified for the world" so "that through him *all* might be saved" (76:41–42; emphasis added). In this way, Christ "glorifies the Father, and saves *all* the works of his hands, except those sons of perdition" (76:43; emphasis added).

This is what true victory looks like: Christ saves *all* the works of his hands.

Everyone goes to heaven.[11]

"This is the gospel," Joseph and Sidney testify, "the glad tidings, which the voice out of the heavens bore record unto us" (76:40).

And this, as Paul puts it, is how Christ fulfills God's plan so that "God may be all in all" (1 Corinthians 15:28).

Christ triumphs only once all is in all.

This, of course, is not to deny that different heavenly kingdoms can vary, perhaps dramatically, "in glory as the moon differs from the sun" or "as the glory of the stars differs from that of the glory of the moon" (76:78, 81). But it is, I think, to emphatically deny that all these different degrees of glory are anything but—really, truly— kingdoms of *heaven*. Even the "glory of the telestial . . . surpasses all understanding" (76:89).

Christ has conquered both death and sin. And, so, all of heaven's gates are now unlocked. All of heaven's doors are wide open. All of heaven's walls have been leveled. All of heaven's borders stand undefended.

And in light of section 76, heaven's different degrees of glory no longer mark anything like how far anyone is *allowed* to go in these new worlds. Rather, they mark how far we're *willing* to go.

But, then, the crucial question is just this: how far *am* I willing to go? And how far am I willing to go doing . . . what?

These different degrees of glory mark, I think, how far I'm willing to go in living and loving—forever—in the same glorious, selfless, sacrificial way that God lives and loves. Only an unconditional commitment to love's work can fit me "to bear his presence in the world of glory" (76:118).

In this spirit, we might frame one way of describing what's at stake in these different degrees of glory simply in terms of what section 76 calls "ministering."

We will inherit whatever degree of glory best corresponds to however far we're willing to go in our efforts to love and minister. We will inherit whatever kingdom best corresponds to however much of God's love and glory we're willing to bear and share.

In a fascinating pair of verses that come late in the section, we're told that those who inherit a telestial glory are "they who receive not of [Christ's] fulness in the eternal world, but of the Holy Spirit through the ministration of the terrestrial; and the terrestrial through the ministration of the celestial" (76:86–87). Here, the differences between these kingdoms are marked in terms of ministering. Those in the celestial kingdom minister to those in the terrestrial kingdom. And those in the terrestrial kingdom minister to those in the telestial kingdom.

These gradations of glory, then, seem to correspond to different degrees of activity or passivity in ministering. Those who inherit a celestial glory actively and unconditionally minister to others. Those who inherit a terrestrial glory sometimes passively receive ministering and sometimes actively minister to others. Their ministering is conditional. Those who inherit a telestial glory simply and passively receive ministering without ministering themselves. And those consigned to darkness are those who refuse ministry of any kind—active or passive, unconditional or conditional.

With respect to different degrees of postmortal glory, the decisive question might simply be this: How much do I love ministering? How much ministering am I willing to do?

If I love ministering the way God loves ministering, then I'll see the world the way God does. I'll go where God is. I'll live as God lives. I'll inherit the fulness of this ministerial work.

"And thus we saw the glory of the celestial, which excels in all things—where God, even the Father, reigns upon his throne forever and ever," where "they who dwell in his presence are the church of the Firstborn; and they see as they are seen, and know as they are known, having received of his fulness and of his grace" (76:92, 94).

This is exaltation: fearless in love, I'm finally willing to see as I'm seen and know as I'm known. My eyes have been touched. My blindness has healed. My mind is now willing.

Adam

> "For all the rest shall be brought forth by the resurrection of the dead, through the triumph and the glory of the Lamb, who was slain, who was in the bosom of the Father before the worlds were made." (Doctrine and Covenants 76:39)

Adam,

You describe heaven as a particular kind of love shared with God, and I think that's exactly right: "Fearless in love, I'm finally willing to see as I'm seen and know as I'm known." One metaphor for exaltation might be the exchange of gazes with one you love—trustful, receptive, candid, still. Everything is known in that look, and everything is disclosed. The substance of the celestial promise is this entrance into direct, intimate communion with God and the infusion of courage it takes to walk through that open door. And then, as you say, with eternity in their eyes, the exalted ones turn the same ministering gaze on others. Trustful, receptive, candid, still.

This section adds another iconic scriptural vision of Christ to those in the revelations we've already read. In section 19 we saw him shrinking in agony yet not ceasing to return glory to the Father. In section 45 we saw him clothed in glory descending among the clouds of heaven. And here in section 76 we see the ascended Christ "crowned with the crown of his glory, [seated] on the throne of his power to reign forever and ever" (76:108).

It's worth lingering over this throne for a moment. Christ's throne represents his authority, power, majesty, and splendor as the ascended Lord. The heavenly throne represents the high seat of divine glory—which, as we saw in our first chapter, is the energy that emanates from God's presence as brilliance that inaugurates and sustains all earthly creation as light and that returns from earth to heaven as praise. We don't get much description of the throne itself in section 76, but elsewhere in scripture the divine throne is described with spectacular metaphors like flaming fire (see Daniel 7:9), glittering sapphires (see Ezekiel 1:26), and bolts of lightning (see Revelation 4:5). This throne practically begs for visual representation—which is perhaps why it's been the center of so many visions of God.

The throne of God will always be the image I mentally connect to Doctrine and Covenants 76. But there's more to this vision than majesty and magnificence. The revelation interweaves its spectacular scenes with intimate beats. In fact, the throne itself has an intimate dimension of meaning: God's throne affirms his kingship and symbolizes his kingdom, and the kingdom of God is both magnificent *and* personal. Yes, it's the ultimate wedding party, as we saw in section 45's reference to the parable of the bridegroom and the virgins. Or, in the imagery of section 76, the kingdom of God "surpass[es] all understanding in glory, and in might, and in dominion" (76:114). But Christ also teaches about the kingdom in another way: "the kingdom of God is within you," he says (Luke 17:21). "Blessed are the poor in spirit: for theirs is the kingdom of heaven" (Matthew 5:3). Whatever else it is, exaltation is also an intimate, inward state of mind, the "mind . . . which was also in Christ Jesus" (Philippians 2:5).

So if Christ's spectacular throne represents the glory, might, and dominion of his kingship, it shouldn't be surprising that Doctrine and Covenants 76 gives us another, more personal image of Christ's seat that represents the inward kingdom. The phrase "in the bosom of the Father" appears three times in this section (76:13, 25, 39). The image of Christ in the Father's bosom echoes the opening of the Gospel of John, where "the only begotten Son" is pictured in the same way, "in the bosom of the Father" (John 1:18). This verse is sampled repeatedly in Doctrine and Covenants 76, and I think it's a key to understanding Joseph's vision of Christ and the Father.

The root of the biblical word *bosom* refers to "the upper part of the chest where a garment naturally folded to form a 'pocket' . . . , the position synonymous with intimacy."[12] A vision of Christ "in the bosom of the Father" shows the Son in the closest physical contact with the Father—sitting in his lap or leaning into his side. It conveys Christ's unmatched union with our Father and the tender quality of the love they share: "the Only Begotten Son whom the Father loved . . . was in the bosom of the Father" (76:25). In fact, the corresponding Hebrew word is used in the Old Testament to describe Naomi's tender care for her grandson, Ruth's child. Ruth herself represents the close generational loyalty between parent and child. After Ruth gave birth to little Obed, "Naomi took the child, and laid it in her bosom, and became nurse unto it" (Ruth 4:16).

When my first child was born, my world nearly wobbled off its axis. In those early days, while sleep deprivation and postpartum hormones rampaged in my brain, I came to the sure conclusion that I could not be trusted to keep this child alive. The only reasonable course of action was to give up my new baby to my mother, who had borne and raised eleven children of her own. Only there, in the bosom that had nurtured me, would my child be safe. I decamped in desperation to my parents' home, seeking my mother's arms for myself as much as for my baby.

My wise mother knew that I could care for my little one on my own, once my body and brain got stronger. She gave me a brown corduroy sling she had sewn herself to carry her own babies—a modern version of the chest pocket envisaged by the Greek word for *bosom*. It's little exaggeration to say that this humble scrap of fabric is responsible for the survival of my first child and my willingness to bear three more. With my child wrapped close in my bosom, she calmed and slept, and, in the weeks and months that followed,

I came to myself. The storms of anxiety subsided, mastered by a threadbare brown baby carrier.

There's a reason so many mothers say their newborn's head smells like heaven. The feeling of surpassing at-oneness I get when a baby rests in the rise and fall of my breath is to me a foretaste of the celestial condition. Section 76 describes this surpassing heaven as nested states of belonging: "all things are theirs, whether life or death, or things present, or things to come, all are theirs and they are Christ's, and Christ is God's" (76:59). The imagery of God's parental bosom brings into the text a mother's—or grandmother's or aunt's—tenderness, a welcome softness in the exhilarating scriptural imagery that otherwise celebrates male figures and a masculine ambiance. (It also, of course, affirms that tenderness and intimacy are prized qualities of divine masculinity.)

And there's a theological upshot, in addition to the emotional punch. On a practical and physiological level, what makes close contact between mother and child feel so satisfying is that it reunites two bodies that very recently were one. My child lived within me— or *indwelt* me, in theological language—for thirty-eight weeks. Holding her to my bosom returns us (nearly!) to that state of bodily oneness, our undivided coregulation and coperception. This is why scholars interpret John 1:18, the evocative verse sampled so often in Doctrine and Covenants 76, to show Christ "in the bosom of the Father" as a representation of the oneness of the Godhead. Christ shares in the innermost heart and mind of the Father. Jesus would later describe the bosom of God in this way: "I am in the Father, and the Father in me" (John 14:11). Jesus teaches us that celestial exaltation is our own realization of his inward oneness with the heart of God. We're closing in, maybe, on the particular kind of love that created earth in the beginning and creates heaven in the now.

If the Savior's unity with the Father shows us heaven as a certain kind of love, it also recasts revelation in the same way. After placing

Christ in the bosom of the Father, John 1:18 goes on to state that Jesus Christ "has made [the Father] known" (John 1:18, NRSV). Christ *himself* is a revelation: the greatest revelation of all, the revelation of God. This is what President Jeffrey R. Holland meant when he taught that "in word and in deed Jesus was trying to reveal and make personal to us the true nature of His Father, our Father in Heaven."[13] The image in section 76 of Christ resting in the rise and fall of the Father's breath makes visual what it means that Christ is the revelation of God. It's as if Jesus, in the bosom of the Father, becomes the outward face of God.

Picture my daughter sitting on my lap—it seems a little undignified to imagine Christ sitting in the lap of God, but that's what the image, taken literally, suggests—and see how her face, positioned in front of mine, *becomes* my face to someone standing in front of us. If I could, through love, share with her my perception and my purpose entirely, my child would become my visual avatar. She would reveal me to the world beyond. In the same way, through the shared love of Father and Son figured by image of the divine bosom, Christ, in every word and deed of his premortal, mortal, and postmortal ministries, is the revelation of God's love.

What was the Savior's premortal and postmortal work? John 1 opens with a song of praise to the premortal Christ, the divine Word who was in the bosom of the Father before the creation of the world (see John 1:1–3). The phrase "in the bosom of the Father" likewise shows up in Doctrine and Covenants 76 as a marker for the recurring scene of the premortal council in heaven, in which Lucifer is thrust down and Christ makes the worlds according to God's plan. By contrast, the image of Christ at the throne of God is associated with Christ's postmortal work, his completion of the gathering of God's children on both sides of the veil, "when he shall deliver up the kingdom, and present it unto the Father, spotless" (76:107). But this vision is not a straightforward narrative from beginning to end. It tends to swoop through time, zoom in on a particular scene, reverse course, and revisit themes. The twin images of the bosom and the throne can help track whether we're seeing the beginning or the end of God's work.

And I think something more than chronology becomes clear in the contrast between the bosom and the throne. The two seats of Christ give us two different visions of God's power. The throne is the seat of a king who rules supremely—with supreme excellence, supreme wisdom, supreme strength. The defining feature of a throne is its height, and in the scriptures, as in real life, height communicates power and preeminence to those below. As a kid, did you ever stand on your father's feet and look up to his face towering above, or ride on his shoulders and marvel at the view? The throne sets God and his Christ above creation. In the language of Doctrine and Covenants 76, the Godhead is "the highest of all," secure in its title as "the Most High" (76:70, 112). When exercised from the throne and viewed from below, as I noted earlier, divine power looks to Joseph and Sidney like "glory," "power," "might," and "dominion" (76:91).

But Jesus Christ is the bread of heaven who came down to earth (see John 6:51). He gave up the courts of the Most High, put on a mortal body, and condescended to serve and sanctify the least—or lowest—of God's children, you and me. If Christ was to fully reveal God's love, a throne was never going to adequately seat him. Only the bosom of the Father would do, the unity of divine disposition that Jesus takes with him to whatever depth or distance his ministry requires. And if I'm on the right track in the way I've been reading this symbol, then it gives a very different vision of divine power than we see in the throne.

When exercised from the bosom of the Father and viewed from the position of, say, Joseph Smith and Sidney Rigdon in Kirtland, Ohio, on February 16, 1832, then Christ's means of triumphantly delivering up the kingdom to his Father looks less like sovereign power and more like encircling arms. Divine power that flows from love, not force, is what allows God to save us without violating our agency. Indeed, God meets and nourishes our agency with his. In God's embrace, we unite with him, but we do not lose ourselves; on the contrary, we come to our true selves (see Luke 15:17). In the bosom of the Father, two become "at one"; and thus God's embrace is an "at-one-ment" that preserves agency. This, I think, is what is meant by the nested states of belonging that Joseph and Sidney see in—and as—heaven: "all things are theirs, whether life or death, or things present, or things to come, all are theirs and they are Christ's, and Christ is God's" (76:59).

As you put it, Adam: to triumph, Christ doesn't defeat; he saves.

Maybe my focus on these twin images of the throne and the bosom seems a little beside the point. For good reason, section 76 is remembered mostly for its description of the Prophet's spectacular theophany and for his mind-blowing revelation that salvation is bigger than anything that had been previously contemplated in the Christian world. But I think the image of Christ in the bosom of the Father is more than a passing metaphor, mere decoration for doctrine. In fact, the idea of embracing God shows up again and again in Restoration scripture, bringing with it the truth that God's power to save flows from his love, not his sovereignty. It's not an overstatement to say that the bosom of the Father, and the agentic embrace we find there, is essential to every stage of the plan of salvation.

We've already seen how, drawing on John 1:18, the Father's bosom becomes a symbol of Christ's premortal existence. And because modern revelation teaches that all humans were, with Christ, "also in the beginning with God" (Doctrine and Covenants 93:29), I imagine the same warm intimacy in our own foundational relationship with God. We know that "in the premortal realm, spirit sons and daughters knew and worshipped God as their Eternal Father."[14] Eliza R. Snow's poetic question pictures our premortal relationship with the Creator as the tender bond of parent and small child: "In my first primeval childhood was I nurtured near thy side?"[15] Snow communicates both the literal ("near thy side") and relational ("nurture") meanings of the *bosom of the Father* in her vivid turn of phrase.

We've followed Christ into embodied mortality now, but we need not leave the embrace of the Father. Divine aid is at hand. "I will not leave you comfortless," the Savior promised (John 14:18). And in Restoration scripture, that promised help is represented, again, by the embrace of the Godhead. We see it in the Lord's intimate admonition to Oliver Cowdery: "Behold, thou art Oliver, and I have spoken unto thee because of thy desires. . . . Be faithful and diligent in keeping the commandments of God, and I will encircle thee in the arms of my love" (Doctrine and Covenants 6:20). Just seven years later, Oliver would see Christ unveiled in the Kirtland temple.

Death, too, is an embrace in the bosom of God. Alma taught that "the spirits of all men, as soon as they are departed from this mortal body . . . are taken home to that God who gave them life" (Alma 40:11). Through temple teachings, I've learned to embrace my approaching death as a homecoming, though in this respect I need more practice. I rehearse my passing each time the Lord opens his arms and clasps me to his bosom.

For Latter-day Saints, though, the plan of salvation is bigger than any one person's private return to God's arms. As President Russell M. Nelson put it, "Salvation is an individual matter; exaltation is a family matter."[16] Exaltation is brought to pass by way of sealed relationships that unite the human family. To rest in the bosom of the Father, then, we must open our arms to each other— whether through formal practices like vicarious temple work or through spontaneous daily acts of forgiveness and reconciliation. In one of the most memorable passages of Restoration scripture, the prophet Enoch is shown a vision of God's kingdom as a scene of embrace that clasps all of space and time between reconciled peoples. Echoing the powerful imagery of the reunion between the prodigal son and his father, the Lord says to Enoch: "Then shalt thou and all thy city meet them there, and we will receive them into our bosom, and they shall see us; and we will fall upon their necks, and they shall fall upon our necks, and we will kiss each other; and there shall be mine abode, and it shall be Zion" (Moses 7:63–64).

Christ dwells in the bosom of the Father, rests in the rise and fall of his breath. Once dead, he is alive again. That is the life and the death, and breath and the bosom, to which you and I, too, belong.

Rosalynde

— CHAPTER 4 —

Christic in All Things

DOCTRINE AND COVENANTS 88

In this revelation, the Lord invites all to seek, ask, and knock, and he will unveil his face in his own time and way. Christ is both the vision and the light by which all else is seen because the light of Christ shines in and through all things. True light proceeds from the presence of God to fill the immensity of space and is the renewal and sanctification of creation; Christ's light is the life and law of all kingdoms in their diversity. He who has seen these kingdoms has seen God but will not comprehend it until his quickening. The Lord visits each laborer in his kingdom at the appointed hour.

Preparation to see the face of the Lord includes purification, washing, fasting, praying, teaching, and learning. Calamities and commotion will precede the Saints' receiving their inheritance. The Saints are commanded to organize and prepare needful things and to establish a house of learning, by study and also by faith. The law of the gospel governs this school and sets out godly comportment, order, and the bonds of charity. Learners should greet one another with a holy greeting and wash one another's feet.

Rosalynde,

You have, again, succeeded with one of my favorite interpretive gestures: you've taken two familiar but discrete images and then paired them in a way that feels both surprising and inevitable. Pairing these images, you've quickened them both.

We have section 76's repeated references to Christ as the "Only Begotten Son, who was in the bosom of the Father, even from the beginning" (76:13; see also 76:25, 39). And we have the section's repeated references to Christ being "crowned with the crown of his glory, to sit on the throne of his power to reign forever and ever" (76:108; see also 76:21–23, 110). We have the premortal Son seated on the lap of his Father, and we have the postmortal Son seated on a throne at his Father's right hand, the tender intimacy of the first image intertwined with the triumphant majesty of the second.

Having paired these images, it's hard now not to explicitly add a third—especially in light of your personal reflections—an image that's central to thousands of years of Christian iconography, an image that's also been endlessly recreated in countless paintings, murals, and stained-glass windows: the image of the Christ child seated on Mary's lap, gathered in Mary's arms, cradled in Mary's bosom. "Madonna and child."

Here, the moment of final triumph is revealed, in substance, as a family reunion: the Son gathered into the bosom of his Father and mother. As grand as all those regal images of global conquest may be, the truth about our redemption is ultimately much closer to home—much more local, much more familiar, and much more domestic.

Section 88—an "'olive leaf' . . . plucked from the Tree of Paradise, the Lord's message of peace to us" (section heading)— is another excellent example of this same telescopic fusion of the massive and the mundane, of the infinitely big and the incredibly small.[17]

Section 88, all 141 verses of it, may be the most ambitious, overwhelming, and far reaching of any revelation in the Doctrine and Covenants. It fills all space and folds all time. The revelation came to Joseph Smith and nine others as they prayerfully sought guidance about how to establish Zion. After offering an extended meditation on how the light of Christ fills "the immensity of space," the revelation ultimately transitions into a passionate and practical exhortation to "seek learning, even by study and also by faith" (88:12, 118). Given the depth and breadth of Christ's light, the Saints must "be instructed more perfectly in theory, in principle, in doctrine" (88:78). They must learn "of things both in heaven and in the earth, and under the earth; things which have been, things which are, things which must shortly come to pass; things which are at home, things which are abroad," so that they "may be prepared in all things" (88:79–80). If the kingdom of God is to be realized, the revelation emphasizes, education is key. And if Zion is to be upbuilt, then the Saints badly need a temple-centered "school of the prophets" (88:127).

If *everything* is saturated with Christ's light, the revelation suggests, then our task is straightforward: we must *learn* how to see this light.

Here, the work of redemption is literally the work of enlightenment.

Taken as a whole, section 88 is so big and daunting that it took three days, stretched across more than a week, to be given and received. Joseph and friends convened on December 27, 1832, again on the 28th, and for a third time on January 3, 1833.

Given its reach and complexity, you and I could, I think, devote whole books to carefully reading just this one revelation. But in keeping with our theme of Christic visions, I want to focus on just one facet—what this revelation refers to as "the light of Christ" (88:7).

The section opens with a promise to send the Saints "another Comforter . . . even the Holy Spirit of promise" (88:3). But what promise, exactly, will the Holy Spirit bring as a message of comfort? "This Comforter is the promise which I give unto you of eternal life, even the glory of the celestial kingdom" (88:4).

We've already reflected on the nature of God's "glory," but here the word has a very specific rhetorical function. Here, the revelation's brief invocation of "glory" functions as an irresistible fuse that, once lit, will shortly *explode* into almost fifty soaring, panoramic verses that explore how this glory manifests as the light of Christ— i.e., the very light of truth itself—a light that is "in all and through all things" (88:6).

And when section 88 says "all things," it isn't kidding. It isn't being poetic or hyperbolic. When it says the light of Christ is "in all and through all things," it really means *all* things.

This light of Christ is "in the sun, and the light of the sun"; it's in the moon and the light of the moon; it's in the stars and the light of the stars; it's in this earth on which we stand and in those eyes by which we come to understand (88:7; see also 88:8–11). This light "giveth life to all things" (88:13). Moreover, this light is "the law by which all things are governed, even the power of God who sitteth upon his throne, who is in the bosom of eternity, who is in the midst of all things" (88:13).

Finding myself spellbound by the propulsive and expansive

thrill of these first fifty verses, two different images come to mind that, for me, help capture their soaring spirit.

First, these verses *feel* to me, kinetically, like a steeply pitched free fall down the opening slope of a very tall roller coaster. Reading them, I find my heart is in my throat, my stomach is in knots. I'm lifted out of my seat, squinting, clinging, eyes watering, faint, exhilarated—gripped by elemental forces as the sky rolls away and the earth rushes up to greet me.

But, too, these verses also remind me of that astonishingly clever and beautiful shot that opens one of my favorite movies, *Contact*.

My reasons for loving this movie, I'll confess, are more than cinematic. Gwen and I saw this heady sci-fi classic on our first date in 1997, and for twenty-five years now the film's poster—recovered from the very same lightbox at that very same theater where we first saw the movie—has hung above our bed. Lacking cars, we walked the couple of miles to the theater, down the hill at the south end of BYU's campus, toward the center of Provo, laughing as we hurried to arrive on time. The movie is based on Carl Sagan's novel of the same name. It's about a scientist (played by Jodie Foster) and a theologian (played by Matthew McConaughey) who make first contact. Gwen, you know, is a scientist herself, and even then, even from that first night, the mirrored symmetry of watching that movie together delighted us.

Contact's unbroken opening shot is more than three minutes long. It doesn't involve any actors, any action, or any dialogue. The shot opens with a partial view of Earth from space and then zooms out. And keeps zooming out. And keeps zooming out. Slowly at first. And then faster and faster. The shot pulls back from the earth to include the moon. It pulls back through the asteroid belt, beyond the red glow of Mars, beyond Jupiter's bands and Saturn's rings. Our colossal sun shrinks to a tiny dot as the camera's point of view reaches the edge of our solar system and our planet's weak crackle of radio signals fades to stone-cold silence. And then the shot keeps going. It pans wider and deeper and faster, pulling back past star after star, through nebulae, past the "pillars of creation," bringing into view a dense cluster of stars, an arm of the Milky Way, the glowing eye of that swirling storm, and still farther, impossibly farther, swallowing up whole galaxies and clusters of galaxies and superclusters of galaxies, faster and faster until the edges of the shot begin to blur and the light at the center of the shot begins to bend and the image grows rounded and convex—until finally that blank wall of immense silence is cracked by a tiny human voice, asking again and again if anyone is out there listening—anyone, anywhere—and we see the whole of reality, every planet and every star and every galaxy, reflected in the pupil of a child's eye.

It's a mesmerizing shot.

The first fifty verses of section 88 are, in this same way, sublime.

> He comprehendeth all things, and all things are before him, and all things are round about him; and he is above all things, and in all things, and is through all things, and is round about all things; and all things are by him, and of him, even God, forever and ever. And again, verily I say unto you, he hath given a law unto all things, by which they move in their times and their seasons; and their courses are fixed, even the courses of the heavens and the earth, which comprehend the earth and all the planets. And they give light to each other in their times and in their seasons, in their minutes, in their hours, in their days, in their weeks, in their months, in their years—all these are one year with God, but not with man. The earth rolls upon her wings, and the sun giveth his light by day, and the moon giveth her light by night, and the stars also give their light, as they roll upon their wings in their glory, in the midst of the power of God. (88:41–45)

Overwhelmed by the scale of these verses, it's tempting to set them aside as, at best, an intensely beautiful gift that ultimately has little to do with concrete religious problems like sin and salvation.

But this is exactly the mistake section 88 warns against.

The degree of glory to which I am resurrected, the revelation says, depends entirely on how much light and glory I am willing to "abide" (see 88:22–24).

In the Resurrection, we're told, everyone will simply "enjoy that which they are willing to receive," and if less light and glory are received, it will be "because they were not willing to enjoy that which they might have received" (88:32). "For what doth it profit a man if a gift is bestowed upon him, and he receive not the gift?" (88:33).

As this revelation has it, God has zero reluctance to give this gift to anyone. In fact, in crucial ways, he's *already* giving it to everyone. The problem here is my reluctance to receive it. The problem is my reluctance to love and receive and "enjoy" what God is giving.

The decisive question is this: how much light am I willing to receive and enjoy? How much truth am I willing to bear? How much law am I willing to abide? How wide open are my eyes? How single is my mind?

Being redeemed, we often say, means living in God's presence. But if section 88 is right and God's presence already fills the immensity of space—if that light is already "in all and through all things" (88:6)—then what am I waiting for? These first fifty verses crescendo, quite plainly, with the claim that "*any* man who hath seen *any* or the least of these hath seen God moving in his majesty and power" (88:47; emphasis added).

This is why I think the revelation then pivots so hard toward the necessity of a spiritual education and the need for a school of the prophets. To be saved, I must learn how to see Christ's light and abide God's truth. I must learn how to stop turning away from this light in shame and fear. I must learn how to stop wandering away from the reality God is now giving—beautiful and vast and difficult and redemptive as it is—in favor of vague fantasies rooted in vain desires.

My salvation depends, the revelation says, on learning how to "cleave" rather than flee. "For intelligence cleaveth unto intelligence; wisdom receiveth wisdom; truth embraceth truth; virtue loveth virtue; light cleaveth unto light" (88:40).

What, then, does it look like to cleave rather than flee?

To cleave to the light, my eye must become single.

"And if your eye be single to my glory, your whole bodies shall be filled with light, and there shall be no darkness in you; and that body which is filled with light comprehendeth all things. Therefore, sanctify yourselves that your minds become single to God, and the days will come that you shall see him; for he will unveil his face unto you, and it shall be in his own time, and in his own way, and according to his own will" (88:67–68).

If I'm serious about seeing the face of God—about entering God's presence and seeing the light of Christ in and through all things—I have to learn how to live in just this way. I have to learn how to cleave. I have to learn how to abide in truth. I have to learn how to live with my mind focused and single instead of distracted and divided. I have to stop trying to serve two masters (see Luke 16:13; 3 Nephi 13:24).

Adam

> "The light shineth in darkness, and the darkness comprehendeth it not; nevertheless, the day shall come when you shall comprehend even God, being quickened in him and by him." (Doctrine and Covenants 88:49)

Adam,

I'll see your first-date story and raise you one of my own. Never one for timid gestures, John invited me for our first date to see the opera *Salome*, which is based on the biblical events described in Mark 6. This might sound more staid than saucy until you realize that the show features several head-turning scenes like the "Dance of the Seven Veils" and, yes, John the Baptist's severed skull on a platter. I'm pretty sure John—both mine and the Baptist—expected more Bible and less seduction and murder. But it turned out to be a headbanger of a production, really ahead of its time, and we laughed about it all the way home. Suffice it to say, I was head over heels from that first night.

I love what you've done with section 88. You've built me a few mental models of this section's internal engine, which is helpful as I try to grasp the entirety of its God's-eye perspective. You model the revelation's textual shape as something like a gorgeous bomb, with a short fuse at the beginning leading up to the phrase "glory of the celestial kingdom" in verse 4, whereupon it explodes in light and energy. You model its sensation as a roller coaster, creating the almost-physical effect of rapid weightless expansion that captures, perhaps, something of the eternity of exaltation. And you model its artistry as a cinematic sequence that simultaneously shows us the awe of God's glory and the immersive, intimate state of union with God.

If we were editing a film collage to reflect the moods and themes of section 88, I'd add another clip to your cosmic zoom-out-zoom-in. It's a shot you've seen before in a time-lapse video: a seed stirs, sprouts, sheds its seed coat, and unfurls its tender cotyledon, all in a matter of a few sped-up seconds. The colors are shades of gold and green. The little plant stretches toward the sky, unfolding its secret interior. Its young leaves move to the soundless music of the light and sate the whole world's hunger on sun and water. This, for me, is what it's like to live in the light of Christ.

Section 88 shows that God's presence is in the light that "fills[s] the immensity of space" (88:12). God's light gives itself to everyone everywhere in the energetic radiation that produces and sustains all life. Human lives stir and dance no less than the plant and animal lives that accompany us under the sun. Human and nonhuman communities flourish and make seed from this light. God's work and glory is realized.

I've found that when I can connect a feeling or an image with a passage of scripture, its content sticks long enough to really become part of me. It's a bit like the prophet Ezekiel, who was instructed to eat the scroll of the Torah so that its words would glut his belly, mineralize his bones. He did eat it, he reports, "and in my mouth it was as sweet as honey" (Ezekiel 3:3 NRSV).

As we read section 88, it occurs to me that we may be seeing here, in real time, a turning point in Joseph's prophetic ministry: the dawning understanding that his people didn't need to wait for the Second Coming, didn't need to wait until Zion was built and prospering, to see Christ and enjoy the presence of God. They could build a house for God now and meet him there. This is of course just my own speculation, but maybe what you've noticed about the language of this section—its explosive, exhilarating, immersive quality—tracks Joseph's own exploding prophetic awareness of the meaning of the true light and true life of Christ. It's worth emphasizing the central revelation of this text: "Any man who hath seen any or the least of these [sun, moon, and stars] hath seen God moving in his majesty and power." And then the section immediately reiterates, in case we missed it, "I say unto you, he hath seen him" (88:47–48). How could the text be more emphatic? Joseph and his brothers and sisters *are already in the divine presence.*

When my children were young, I helped them sing, "I am a child of God. . . . Teach me all that I must do to live with him someday."[18] We might read section 88, a text for a grown-up child of God if ever there were one, as a final revised chorus: "Teach me all that I must know: *we live with him today.*" As the short, embedded parable in this section illustrates, the Lord promises that "I will come unto [all], and ye shall behold the joy of my countenance . . . every man in his hour, and in his time, and in his season" (88:52, 58). The light of his countenance falls on every one of us now, already, in our seasons under the sun. It's no wonder the Lord gives his assembled servants a minute to digest this: "I leave these sayings with you to ponder in your hearts" (88:62).

But just as this theological roller coaster picks up speed, it pulls up short: it's possible, the Lord warns, even likely, that, inattentive to the divine light, we will miss the whole thing. We could sleep through our theophany. "Nevertheless, he who came unto his own was not comprehended" (88:48). Again drawing on the great hymn that opens the Gospel of John—an indispensable companion text for these seven visions of Christ, as we've noted—the assembled brothers are reminded that "the light shineth in darkness, and the darkness comprehendeth it not" (88:49). It's not that a dulled mind can't see the light streaming from God in Christ, but it can't comprehend it and, perhaps for that reason, can't be bothered to look for it.

It's hard to imagine that I could ever fail to notice a divine visitation like the ones we're exploring in this book. The dazzling brilliance, the glory—how could anyone miss it? Then again, don't I routinely sleep through the sunrise, drawing the shades, even, to keep out the light? Section 88 is only one of many instances when Christ warns his disciples that most people will simply blink irritably at the divine glory and turn over in bed. Quoting Isaiah, Jesus explained to his disciples why he communicates in parables: "By hearing ye shall hear, and shall not understand; and seeing ye shall see, and shall not perceive: For this people's heart is waxed gross, and their ears are dull of hearing, and their eyes they have closed" (Matthew 13:14–15).

The trick is not just to see, but to see *and perceive.* Later, trudging down the mountain after Christ's transfiguration, when the eyes of the disciples for a moment *did* see and perceive the brilliance of God, they ventured to ask their Master why Elijah hadn't come first to proclaim the imminent arrival of the Messiah, as the scriptures prophesied he would. "Elijah has already come," Jesus answered, "and they did not recognize him" (Matthew 17:12, NRSV).

The constant temptation to suppress our recognition of God in the true light, the light of Christ that is the life of the world, is for me one of the key insights of Doctrine and Covenants 88. We need help learning to comprehend the light that shines in the darkness, and we need help finding the courage to dance under it. Indeed, learning this dance is precisely the point of the temple, the purifying ordinances, the school of the prophets, and everything else that begins right here in section 88.

I wonder, though, if section 88 doesn't also warn against a kind of equal and opposite temptation. If there's real risk of failing to comprehend that *I have seen God* during my own season in the sun of God's presence, there may also be a risk of assuming too much—of assuming that I've already received what section 88 calls "a fulness" of his glory when in reality I've only received "a portion" (88:29). Whether I turn irritably away from the sunrise or mistakenly assume that my basement grow lamp is good enough, the effect is the same: I shut out the true light.

There's a sense of both *already* and *not yet* running through section 88, and through this entire project of exploring the seven visions, in fact. As we've both pointed out in almost every chapter— and as you especially emphasized in your letter on section 19—the Doctrine and Covenants is predicated on the testimony that the Father and Son are no strangers to planet Earth. God is already here. We don't need to wait to eat the sweet fruit of redemption, to rest in the bosom of the Father, to view the glory of the Godhead. God is bathing us in that light *already*.

At the same time, it seems clear that God has *not yet* finished his work in the world. Our latter day is a paradoxical time of completion and futurity, what scholars sometimes call the "overlapping of the ages." It's a time when the kingdom of God and the regime of darkness coexist in the world—but, as we saw in section 76, Christ will not cease saving until his Father's work is finished. In section 88, the Lord laments those who fail to see the light now shining in the darkness but promises, "Nevertheless, the day *shall come* when you *shall comprehend even God, being quickened in him and by him.* Then *shall* ye know that *ye have seen me*, that I am, and that I am the true light that is in you, and that you are in me; otherwise ye could not abound" (88:49–50; emphasis added). The text urges us to recognize God in the present *and* promises that there's a "quickening" yet to come for those who abide God's fulness. That quickening is described here as the future understanding of what we have already seen. The fulness yet to come is a fulness of comprehension. Is that how you read it?

Paul was the first Christian disciple, and perhaps remains the keenest, to understand the "already and not yet" timing of Christ's coming. After all, he had already met the resurrected Christ on the road to Damascus; Christ had already come—to him. And Christ's coming had already raised Paul from the dead by giving him new spiritual life, the rebirth that comes immediately to all those willing to die with Christ in baptism: "If then you have [already] been raised with Christ," Paul exhorts, "seek the things that are above" (Colossians 3:1, NRSV). I think this new spiritual life, the gift of Christ's having already come, is just what section 88 is getting at in its parable of the master who visits each of his servants in turn, wherein each is "made glad with the light of the countenance of his lord" (88:56). And yet Paul simultaneously remains committed, as does section 88, to the teaching that Christ has not yet—but soon will—appear in his kingship and kingdom (see 1 Thessalonians 4:16). As section 88 teaches, at this culminating appearance our "comprehension" of Christ will be made full, and we'll look with new eyes to see that Christ has always and already been with us (see 88:49–50).

So how are the *already* and *not yet* to be reconciled, if at all? Here, too, Paul's teachings and the vision of section 88 work hand in hand. Paul teaches that the Holy Spirit works as a kind of "down payment" on the Second Coming, giving us both the promise and the present experience of the life to come in Christ's kingdom. Christ "anointed us, set his seal of ownership on us," Paul writes, "and put his Spirit in our hearts as a deposit, guaranteeing what is to come" (2 Corinthians 1:21–22, NIV). In the evocative words of the King James translators, Christ has "given the earnest of the Spirit in our hearts" (2 Corinthians 1:22). He has already "purchased" us— we are marked with his seal, and thus we already belong to him. He has put down the "deposit" or "earnest money" of the Holy Spirit as a promise of his full "payment" at the Second Coming. The financial metaphor has its limits, but the point is clear: the present ministering of the Spirit is a foretaste and a sure promise of our culminating belonging in Christ, or "comprehension." The Spirit allows us to skip to the end and live there now.

In his letter to the Ephesians, Paul makes the same point using the phrase "the Holy Spirit of Promise," and it's no coincidence that the same phrase appears early in section 88: "Wherefore, I now send upon you another Comforter, even upon you my friends, that it may abide in your hearts, even the Holy Spirit of promise. . . . This Comforter is the promise which I give unto you of eternal life, even the glory of the celestial kingdom" (88:3–4, compare Ephesians 1:13). One way to read this assurance of "another Comforter . . . , even the Holy Spirit of promise," then, is that the Holy Spirit reconciles two extraordinary teachings in section 88: (1) that the Saints have already seen Christ among them and (2) that the Saints must urgently warn their neighbors that Christ is about to come. The Spirit bridges the *already* with the *not yet* and will, if we allow him in, open our eyes to the ways Christ is already present. Both things are true.

This is the kind of theological tension that is delicious to me as a literary scholar. But it's also just a really good description of what it feels like to try to follow Jesus. He's brought me to life again and again, already. And yet I feel pulled forward toward a quickening and a comprehension that I can't yet fully make out.

It can be hard to hold both feelings at once. As Latter-day Saints, I think we're generally pretty good at the *not yet* part. The very name of our church, which President Russell M. Nelson has emphasized anew, reminds us that, situated as we are in the latter days, we're waiting and working toward the fulness of the kingdom that we call Zion.[19] This gives us an alacrity of cooperative obedience for which we're known, and which I treasure in our people.

Sometimes we're less attuned to the *already*, less able to comprehend and less accustomed to expressing what King Benjamin's people experienced: "this day . . . [we] are born of him" (Mosiah

5:7). This is something that, as a people, we may just be starting to learn from the scriptures of the Restoration, the history of our people, and the life-ministry of our founding prophet.

Still, I'm grateful for the Doctrine and Covenants' simultaneous and insistent *not yet*. I need it to cut through the complacency and self-congratulation I'm often tempted to wallow in. I need it to shake me free from a false life of ceaseless scrabbling for ever greater degrees of convenience and consumption. I am looking for degrees of glory, not degrees of comfort. I'm not there yet.

Rosalynde

— CHAPTER 5 —

The Face of Christ

DOCTRINE AND COVENANTS 110

Joseph Smith and Oliver Cowdery, after dedicating the Kirtland temple, offer silent prayer, and the veil is taken from their minds. They see a vision of the Lord standing on the breastwork of the temple pulpit before them with a shining countenance and mighty voice. The Lord forgives Joseph and Oliver of their sins and accepts the Saints' offering of the Kirtland temple. He promises to put his name in this house and manifest himself to his people there.

Moses appears and commits the keys of the gathering of Israel. Elias appears and commits the dispensation of the gospel of Abraham. Then, Elijah, the prophet, appears and commits the keys of the sealing power. Elijah quotes Malachi on the importance of turning the hearts of the children to their fathers and the hearts of the fathers to their children. By the transfer of these keys, Joseph and Oliver may know that the day of the Lord is at the door.

Rosalynde,

Degrees of glory, not degrees of comfort—I love it.

And, of course, Christ is always both *already* and *not yet*. As Christians we live "look[ing] forward unto the Messiah," even as we also "believe in him to come as though he already was" (Jarom 1:11). Our job as disciples is to live in the truth of this tension.

We've already come a long way. Section 110 brings us, now, to our fifth vision of Christ. And this vision is, at least in part, different in kind.

In section 19, we witnessed Christ shoulder the weight of eternity, "which suffering caused myself, even God, the greatest of all, to tremble because of pain, and to bleed at every pore, and to suffer both body and spirit" (19:18). In section 45, we witnessed Christ returning "in the clouds of heaven, clothed with power" at his second coming (45:44). In section 76, we witnessed Christ "crowned with the crown of his glory," triumphant in his work of redeeming all who are willing, seated "on the throne of his power" (76:108). And in section 88, we witnessed Christ as the light that enlightens our eyes and quickens our understanding, "the light which is in all things, which giveth life to all things" (88:13).

In each case, the images and descriptions have focused on Christ's actions as he suffers, returns, triumphs, or shines. But despite the moving and evocative qualities of these visions, we have not, to this point, been given any actual descriptions of Christ. While the scenes are often strikingly composed and their settings vividly rendered, we're never told what we would see were we to see Christ himself. Despite section 88's promise that if "your minds become single to God," then "the days will come that you shall see him; for he will unveil his face unto you," we're never told what he looks like (88:68).

This is not unusual. Across the whole of scripture, any kind of physical description of Christ is extremely rare. For example, we have four distinct but overlapping accounts of Christ's mortal life and ministry—Matthew, Mark, Luke, and John—and collectively, in their detailed entirety, they don't include a single verse that describes his appearance.

The one thing the Gospels may allow us to reliably infer about his appearance is that, evidently, there was nothing remarkable about his appearance. If you didn't already know him, you'd have trouble picking him out of a crowd. Or if you were a Roman soldier assigned to arrest him, you'd need someone to point him out.

This wholesale absence of any physical description is surely not an accident. And, in a number of obvious ways, it's also surely appropriate and productive. After all, section 88 also promises that when Christ does finally unveil his face to us, "it shall be in his own time, and in his own way, and according to his own will" (88:68).

But still, I want to preserve the idea that it may be both possible and important to encounter Christ as a real person—with a body that is uniquely his own, with a face that is different from every other, with a height and posture that, beyond the brilliance of any divine glory, bear the singular and idiosyncratic stamp of his own experiences, feelings, relationships, and circumstances.

So, at one level, I'm entirely on board with the claim that, with respect to how the light of Christ saturates the whole of creation, "any man who hath seen any or the least of these hath seen God" (88:47). But on another level, especially as a Latter-day Saint, I can't entirely let go of the idea that seeing the face of God must also, at some point, involve actually *meeting* God. (Here, again, we have this same tension between the *already* and the *not yet*.)

It might be true that, in general, I've always been prone to take everything about my religion too literally—or, better, too materially. But I don't think that, in this ambition, I'm alone.

I want to see the face of God.

Section 110, then, offers something that is of great interest to me, something we haven't yet seen in these visions: a description of Christ's appearance.

The date is Sunday, April 3, 1836. This date coincides with both our Christian celebration of Easter and a traditional Jewish celebration of Passover. The place is the newly dedicated Kirtland temple (see Doctrine and Covenants 109).

The section heading included in our scriptures helpfully frames the vision's setting in Joseph Smith's own words: "In the afternoon, I assisted the other Presidents in distributing the Lord's Supper to the Church, receiving it from the Twelve, whose privilege it was to officiate at the sacred desk this day. After having performed this service to my brethren, I retired to the pulpit, the veils being dropped, and bowed myself, with Oliver Cowdery, in solemn and silent prayer. After rising from the prayer, the following vision was opened to both of us."

The whole of section 110 is just sixteen verses long. The first ten verses narrate a vision of Christ himself, seven of which record what he said. The final six verses narrate successive visions of Moses, Elias, and Elijah, together with the delivery of their respective keys and mandates.

The vision opens, quite abruptly and without preamble, as follows: "The veil was taken from our minds, and the eyes of our understanding were opened. We saw the Lord standing upon the breastwork of the pulpit, before us" (110:1–2).

Here, again, it seems that the Lord is not seen coming from

someplace else to appear to Joseph and Oliver. He doesn't suddenly "arrive" and surprise them with his entrance. Rather, once the veil is removed from their minds, they find that he's *already* standing there on the pulpit, already present with them, already waiting for them to open their eyes and see his face. His previous invisibility doesn't seem to be a problem caused by any distance or absence on his part; rather, the problem is Joseph and Oliver's minds. The problem is the "veil" that, under normal conditions, blinkers our ability to see what's already there.

(What exactly is this veil? How is it "taken" from one's mind? And what pair of questions could be more urgent than these? More than a kind of blanket mortal amnesia, Doctrine and Covenants 88:68 and Matthew 6:22–34 together suggest that this veil is drawn specifically by my failure to have a mind that is "single" to the glory of God. That is, this veil is an effect that follows from my default mental attitude of trying to serve more than one master and, thus, from how my mind is continually divided against itself by my tendency to worry about tomorrow. A mind that is divided in this way, we might say, has truly been partitioned by a "veil.")

With this veil removed and the Lord's presence made manifest, section 110 then records the full description of Christ's appearance given by Joseph and Oliver. This description spans two verses (110:2–3), includes two separate sentences, and consists of sixty-nine words. I've taken the liberty of adding line breaks below.

> We saw the Lord standing upon the breastwork of the pulpit, before us;
> And under his feet was a paved work of pure gold, in color like amber.
> His eyes were as a flame of fire;
> The hair of his head was white like the pure snow;
> His countenance shone above the brightness of the sun;

And his voice was as the sound of the rushing of great waters.

This, of course, is nothing like a normal physical description. You couldn't use it to develop a police sketch or search for a missing person. But as gloriously poetic and overexposed as it may be, it nonetheless develops an image that offers *something* like a physical description.

Let's take a quick inventory of this description's key features.

The first sentence offers an indirect description of the Lord's appearance. The Lord stands as a figure above them. Rather than floating or standing directly on the pulpit itself, he stands on a paved work of pure gold, in color like amber. His feet are visible.

The next sentence unfolds as a direct description, primarily by way of similes, of four of the Lord's features, three visual and one aural: his eyes, his hair, his face, and his voice. These descriptions compare him to fire, snow, light, and water.

His eyes are like a flame of fire.

His hair is white like pure snow.

His countenance (i.e., his facial expression) shines brighter than the sun.

His voice sounds like the rushing of great waters.

The first, second, and fourth descriptions are clearly similes: eyes *as* fire, hair *like* snow, voice *as* rushing waters. The third description, though, isn't obviously framed as a simile. Rather, it relies on contrasting levels of brightness: the brightness of the Lord's facial expression is contrasted with the brightness of the sun. This contrast might involve some heightened hyperbole—despite his brightness, the Lord seems to be visible, whereas the sun is typically so bright that a person cannot see anything at all when looking directly at it—but it might not. Maybe visions of this kind simply work differently from our normal vision. But if the comparison does involve some hyperbole, then this description may still function, at least in spirit, like the other three similes, with the contrast really just being an indirect form of poetic alignment: his face shone like (but even brighter than) the sun.

As is often the case in the Doctrine and Covenants, the language repurposed here is borrowed directly from the King James Bible. Section 110's description is modeled on another famous description given in the first chapter of the book of Revelation, where John the Revelator sees the Lord in vision.

> And I turned to see the voice that spake with me. And being turned, I saw seven golden candlesticks; and in the midst of the seven candlesticks one like unto the Son of man, clothed with a garment down to the foot, and girt about the paps with a golden girdle. His head and his hairs were white like wool, as white as snow; and his eyes were as a flame of fire; and his feet like unto fine brass, as if they burned in a furnace; and his voice as the sound of many waters. And he had in his right hand seven stars: and out of his mouth went a sharp twoedged sword: and his countenance was as the sun shineth in his strength. (Revelation 1:12–16)

We're given additional details in this instance about a robe, a golden girdle, a two-edged sword, and hair like wool. But the main outlines are the same: the hair as white as snow, the eyes like a flame of fire, a countenance like the sun, and a voice like the sound of many waters. Section 110 intensifies the "sound of many waters" to a "rushing of great waters," and it intensifies a countenance like the sun to a countenance that shines "above" the brightness of the sun. But the most significant difference seems to be in the description of the feet. Where John describes the Lord's feet as being like fine brass, Joseph and Oliver describe the Lord's feet as standing on a surface like pure gold. The latter, though, does not describe the feet themselves.

We're left to ask: do these descriptions actually tell us anything meaningful about what Jesus, as a person, looks like?

I don't know.

They seem, in principle, more visionary and prophetic than material. And in this way, they likely belong to the same basic category as Isaiah's own prophetic sketch in Isaiah 53. Christians have long read Isaiah's prophecy about a "suffering servant" as a messianic type that refers—ultimately, if not exclusively—to Christ. And if that's the case, then Isaiah's description of this suffering servant might also interest us:

> Who hath believed our report? and to whom is the arm of the Lord revealed? For he shall grow up before him as a tender plant, and as a root out of a dry ground: he hath no form nor comeliness; and when we shall see him, there is no beauty that we should desire him. He is despised and rejected of men; a man of sorrows, and acquainted with grief: and we hid as it were our faces from him; he was despised, and we esteemed him not. (Isaiah 53:1–3)

Again, the tenor of the description is not only prophetic but also poetic. Isaiah is literally writing poetry. And, again, the language consists mostly of similes shaped to heighten and intensify points of contrast. The suffering servant is like a tender shoot rooted in dry ground. He has no form, comeliness, or beauty that we should desire him. Or, as the New English Translation more clearly renders verse two, this suffering servant has "no stately form or majesty that might catch our attention, no special appearance that we should want to follow him."

Could we say, then, that this passage tells us anything meaningful about what Jesus looked like?

I don't know.

If it does, the description certainly pulls in the opposite direction from what we find in Revelation 1 and Doctrine and Covenants 110. Far from being radiant and glorious and overwhelming, the suffering servant's appearance is defined by his vulnerability, by his lack of beauty and majesty.

We might simply account for Isaiah 53's divergence from Doctrine and Covenants 110 in terms of the differences between a mortal body and a resurrected body. And it wouldn't, I think, be impossible to combine the two accounts: someone lacking in what we define as "beauty"—a category which is itself, historically speaking, far from a stable target—could still have, in the Resurrection, eyes aflame with fire, hair white like snow, and a voice like water roaring down a steep and narrow canyon.

One thing, though, that I like about Isaiah 53 is that, for my part, I don't see any reason why Christ couldn't defy *all* our conventional expectations about what does and doesn't count as "beautiful." In fact, it might be a much safer bet to assume that Christ *will* defy all of the world's conventional expectations about beauty.

Were I to see his face, I suspect two things might happen simultaneously: I might both recognize him immediately and, at the same time, still be profoundly surprised by how sharply he diverged from anything I'd anticipated.

In her excellent book *What Did Jesus Look Like?*, historian Joan E. Taylor reviewed two thousand years' worth of Christian images depicting Christ and found essentially that, in every age, we all just fashion Jesus after our own image.[20] Contemporary images, rooted in the dominance of the European tradition, typically depict Jesus as tall and handsome with long fair hair, a beard, a square jaw, blue eyes, and light skin. In other words, our European images present him as a quintessentially White European. Byzantine images present him as the "cosmocrator," robed and enthroned with the Eastern flair of a long, flowing beard. Second- and third-century Christians, competing with Greek and Roman ideas about God, depicted Jesus as slight, youthful, and beardless, with long curly hair—just like Apollo or Dionysus. Other models for his artistic rendering include everything from Moses with his staff to ascetic philosophers too concerned with truth and wisdom—and much too critical of wealth and power—to care about their clothes or combing their hair.

Of course, the flipside of our tendency to fashion Jesus in our own image—and, thus, the flipside of practically all these drawings and paintings—is that our depictions tend to wholly ignore the basic and now widely acknowledged historical facts about Jesus's time, place, and ethnicity.

If, though, we looked at what the Jewish men of Jesus's world typically looked like, what might we say? What might we expect to see? Clement William Grene helpfully summarizes Taylor's findings on this score:

> As the average Middle Eastern Jew, Jesus would have had olive skin and black hair, which he would have worn short, as was customary for men of this period (long hair, like full beards, was reserved for the gods). His stubbly beard would have been the product of neglect, not a deliberate style choice. He would most likely have been 5'5" in height, the average height of the skeletons from the Qumran cemetery. His build would have been slender, not through ascetic choice (Jesus was known to enjoy eating and drinking when he got the chance) but because of his wandering life, although his manual profession may have given him some muscle.[21]

In sum: dark eyes, short dark hair, a short beard, a darker complexion, thin, and quite short by contemporary standards. (If this is accurate, then I would need to imagine standing nearly a foot taller than the Son of God—and, in turn, I would need to recalibrate my expectations for the logistics of that first hug!)

Does this kind of historical work tell us anything meaningful about the face of God?

Maybe.

At the very least, it confirms two things for me.

First, it redoubles my desire to continually join the Psalmist in one of his most powerful prayers: "One thing have I desired of the Lord, that will I seek after; that I may dwell in the house of the Lord all the days of my life, to behold the beauty of the Lord, and to inquire in his temple. . . . When thou saidst, Seek ye my face; my heart said unto thee, Thy face, Lord, will I seek. Hide not thy face far from me" (Psalm 27:4, 8–9).

Thy face, O Lord, I seek; hide not thy face far from me.

And, second, these reflections generally confirm my intuition about the nature of the obstacle that veils my mind and blinds me to God: I don't see the face of God because I tend to force everything I see to fit my own image.

My mind is veiled by its default insistence that everything in the world is for me and about me, that everything in the world must be fashioned in the image of my own will and my own desires and my own expectations. And this insistence is *so* strong, I'm often unable to see anything beyond it.

In truth, this veil can only be lifted by doing what section 76 has already commanded. Rather than fashioning the Lord in my own image, I must be refashioned in his. To see him, I must come to have his image in my countenance. I must come to see everything and everyone the way *he* sees me.

Those who see the face of God are those who are finally able to "see as they are seen, and know as they are known" (Doctrine and Covenants 76:94).

Adam

> "I have accepted this house, and my name shall be here."
> (Doctrine and Covenants 110:7)

Adam,

> *Jesus, the very thought of thee*
> *With sweetness fills my breast;*
> *But sweeter far thy face to see*
> *And in thy presence rest.*[22]

Your desire to see the face of Jesus puts you in company with an ancient fellowship of Jesus-seekers. This poem, one of the oldest texts in our hymnbook, expresses the same longing in the heart of a medieval monk and mystic almost a thousand years ago. It never fails to blow my mind that, through the medium of writing, we commune with the dead.

You and I love the same kinds of novels. Almost ten years ago, we started reading together a series of Norwegian novels, *My Struggle*. Early in the first volume, there's a moment where the boy protagonist, Karl Ove, sees a television news report about a rescue at sea. In the grainy pattern of the televised waves, he discerns the image of a human face. Transported, he runs to tell his father what he's discovered. His father responds dismissively and denies what Karl thinks he's seen: "Now let's not be hearing any more about that face." For the adult Karl remembering this moment, it crystallizes his enduring preoccupation, his "struggle," which is really a question about the possibility of knowing God.[23] Can we discern the face of God in the random informational chaos that threatens to crash over us—the pixelated waves he saw on the television screen? Was his father right that our search for a divine reality beyond the locked-in secular world is just a childish projection of our own imagined image into the fathomless distance?

Yes, his father was probably right about the face in the waves. As you say, we mistake the face of God when we interpret everything we see in our own image. But what I love about the novels is that Karl Ove never gives up his hunch that there *is* something deeper in (and deeper than) the sea. He remains inexhaustibly—though, sometimes, for readers, exhaustingly—receptive to the world and observant of its open patterns. Though his father's scorn erased the face from the sea, the novelist Karl still looks into the fjords as if to find his own countenance there.

Your ruminations on seeing the face of Christ helped me connect two ideas that I've never really considered together, despite their obvious intersection: the *image* of Christ and the *presence* of Christ. It's squarely here—where the revelation of the visual image of Christ meets the experience of being in his presence—that our seven visions come together with their cloud of witnesses. And maybe it's this joint revelation of the image of God and the presence of God that produces the characteristic quality that we've noticed over and over in these texts: their fusion of the overwhelming and the intimate, of the infinitely big and the incredibly small.

If I were to sum up what I've learned so far from this project of deeply reading Joseph's visions, I think I'd say something like this: first, to be in the presence of God is to feel my own nothingness before God's omnipresent, overwhelming glory. In other words, to be in the presence of God is to be unmade and remade in *his* image.

Conversely, I am made in the image of God—in particular, I am made with the power to love as God loves—and that is what enables me to abide his presence. The self-giving, other-oriented aspect of divine love, which I can develop as an inheritance of my divine nature, is what gives me hope that I might escape mere self-projection and *truly* see the face of Christ, in his own image, even as he sees me.

This rare collision of nothingness and mutuality is captured in the phrase from section 76 that you've highlighted a few times now: "They who dwell in his presence . . . see as they are seen, and know as they are known" (76:94). As I said before, these words feel like they belong in a wedding vow. They evoke a love so unmasked, so unmaking, that it really can only be practiced in a relationship sealed by Christ—or in the bosom of God.

In this light, I see section 110 as, symbolically, the first temple wedding of the latter days.

Christ's arrival in the house of the Lord is the realization of the allegorical wedding of the Bridegroom Christ and his Bride, the Church. It's the culmination of the mutual promises and the mutual love that the Savior has taught the Church (here personified by Joseph and Oliver) in each of the previous texts we've read. In section 88, Christ instructed his Church to "draw near unto me and I will draw near unto you; seek me diligently and ye shall find me; ask, and ye shall receive; knock, and it shall be opened unto you" (88:63). She has asked, sought, knocked: the Saints built a house of the Lord and prayed without ceasing. She has drawn near: just that afternoon, the Church gathered to celebrate the sacrament of the Lord's Supper. And then it happens, just as Christ had promised in section 88: "Behold, and lo, the Bridegroom cometh" to his beloved, in the temple she has built for him (88:92).

The idea that God and his people are like a groom and bride bound by covenant is a figurative through line connecting Old Testament, New Testament, and Restoration scripture. Israelite prophet-poets depicted the relationship between God and Israel in marital terms—all too often, alas, in unhappy marital terms (see Hosea 1:2). More festively, as we've just seen in section 45's reference to the parable of the ten virgins, Christ speaks of himself as the triumphant Bridegroom arriving at his wedding feast, the joyous culmination of the kingdom of heaven (see Doctrine and Covenants 45:56; see also Matthew 25:1–13).

But it's in the book of Revelation that the allegorical marriage of Christ and the Church is imagined in its full splendor and joy. As you've pointed out, Adam, the description of Christ in section 110 owes much to the stunning vision of Christ that opens Revelation. What closes that book is an equally stunning vision of New Jerusalem, the Church, descending as the Bride, arrayed in white to meet her Bridegroom.

> Then I heard what sounded like a great multitude, like the roar of rushing waters and like loud peals of thunder, shouting:
> "Hallelujah!
> For our Lord God Almighty reigns.
> Let us rejoice and be glad
> and give him glory!
> For the wedding of the Lamb has come,
> and his bride has made herself ready.
> Fine linen, bright and clean,
> was given her to wear." . . .
> Then the angel said to me, "Write this: Blessed are those who are invited to the wedding supper of the Lamb!" (Revelation 19:6–9, NIV)

This is magnificent, miraculous stuff. The older I've gotten, the more I've come to feel that marriage—every decently happy marriage—is an absolute miracle. Anytime two people manage to overcome the hostile counterwinds in our fraying, narcissism-addled, consumption-obsessed society, anytime they push through the nonsense and come together and learn to love each other and commit to give themselves to each other forever—I'll join the Revelator's "great multitude" in shouting "Hallelujah!" As over-the-top as the imagery in Revelation can seem, I say it's hardly adequate for such a miracle.

And as it happens, Revelation's vision of the wedding supper of the Lamb works perfectly as a duet with section 110. In Revelation, the voice like "rushing waters" issues not from Christ, but from his people, as though the Bride were answering her Bridegroom's joyous shout from across the canon of scripture. Setting these visions next to each other, section 110 lights up as a temple—and especially as a temple *wedding*—text.

In both passages, we see Christ and his Bride dressed in wedding robes. Clean and arrayed in white for one another, he shines in the whiteness of snow (see 110:3) and she in bright linen (see Revelation 19:8). She, at least, is beautiful and "beautifully dressed for her husband" (Revelation 21:2). As for him—you make a good case that "Christ will defy all of the world's conventional expectations about beauty." Still, though, I think we have to read these texts as showing us a Christ who, if not a Norwegian heartthrob, nevertheless is deeply *desirable*. He draws us to himself not with force but by appealing to our highest desires. Section 110's description of Christ shining with the brilliance of fire, snow, and sun is, I think, meant to convey a divine power that attracts our desire and devotion rather than coerces it.

Maybe it's worth noting that, as in these two visions of Christ, almost all scriptural language works on a level beyond the simple communication of meaning. President Dallin H. Oaks taught that, when we read scripture with the Spirit, the text "guide[s] us on things other than simply the meaning of what we're reading."[24] As he goes on to say, scripture is a medium for revelation—above all, the revelation of God himself, through the person of his Only Begotten Son. And to succeed in revealing God, scriptural language must use every tool in its kit to fire our imagination, emotion, aspiration, and desire. Lehi's dream of the shining fruit is an especially powerful example of scripture at work in this way:

I did go forth and partake of the fruit thereof; and I beheld that it was most sweet, above all that I ever before tasted. Yea, and I beheld that the fruit thereof was white, to exceed all the whiteness that I had ever seen. And as I partook of the fruit thereof it filled my soul with exceedingly great joy; wherefore, I began to be desirous that my family should partake of it also; for I knew that it was desirable above all other fruit. (1 Nephi 8:11–12)

It's no coincidence that Lehi's vision of Christ as the sweet, shining fruit shares imagery of brilliance and desire with section 110's resplendent Bridegroom.

Let's get back to that wedding duet. In both texts, Bride and Groom belong to one another, but the wedding party includes multitudes. Joy opens up their private dyad and overflows in widening circles: "Blessed are they which are called unto the marriage supper of the Lamb" (Revelation 19:9); "yea the hearts of thousands and tens of thousands shall greatly rejoice in consequence of the blessings which shall be poured out" (Doctrine and Covenants 110:9). Joy's dramatic expansion is especially clear in section 110: joy expands from Christ alone (who, as you smartly noticed, seems to have gotten there first); to Christ with Joseph and Oliver, together representing the Church; to "all my people" who helped to build the house of the Lord in Kirtland (110:6); to "thousands and tens of thousands" (110:9); to the unbounded reaches of "foreign lands" (110:10). And even this expanded frame is only "the beginning of the blessing" (110:10)!

Temples are working micromodels of the expanding universe, and marriages performed inside them possess the same expansive potential: each union of two contains within it a local eternity of ramifying, redemptive relationships. Like the nuclear fusion that powers the stars, the essential mystery of marriage—two becoming two-as-one—is the source of a creative energy sufficient to turn hearts, link generations, and pressure inject eternity into time.

Section 110's vision of Christ as the allegorical Bridegroom, though predating the full revelation of Latter-day Saint temple marriage theology, already hints at how temples infuse eternity into the here and now: through the energy-generating potentialities of marriage.

Weddings, of course, are only "the beginning of the blessing" of marriage (Doctrine and Covenants 110:10). The real work and real growth happen when bride and groom set up housekeeping together. The cradle of marriage's cosmic creative power is the mundane domestic arrangements entailed in two people eating, sleeping, washing, praying, and breathing in the same space—committed to doing it, in love, forever and ever. Accordingly, both of our texts show the Bridegroom coming home to his Bride to live with her in love. The Revelator reports that "I heard a loud voice from the throne saying, 'Look! God's dwelling place is now among the people, and he will dwell with them. They will be his people, and God himself will be with them and be their God'" (Revelation 21:3, NIV). In section 110, Christ himself announces that he's moving in: "I have accepted this house, and my name shall be here; and I will manifest myself to my people in mercy in this house" (110:7).

If section 110 is the fulfillment of the promise offered directly in section 88—the promise of life in the divine presence, here and now, that's been so carefully developed over each of the sections we've read together—then verse 7 in section 110 is the fulfillment of that fulfillment. Christ has come to dwell directly with his people, in unhindered covenant relationship. Divine presence is no longer remote or abstract but something lived and tangible.

And maybe this is the place where our two readings come together. In some ways, we've taken section 110 in opposite directions: you toward the literal possibility of seeing the face of Christ with unveiled eyes; I toward the literary allegory of Christ's nuptial union with the Church. But when we read scripture *as scripture*— not as science, as fiction, or, indeed, as science-fiction—"literal" and "literary" aren't opposites. Both words share the same Latin root that means "letter." Both approaches pay close attention to the actual words (and letters) on the page. Careful exploration of the figurative aspects of literary language is itself a "literal" interpretation because it remains exquisitely faithful to the "letter" of text, the nuts-and-bolts mechanics of its language.

But most importantly, any approach to scripture, whether literal or literary, is faithful only to the extent that it ends by remaking *me* in the image of God that I encounter in its pages—not the other way round. What you said about seeing Christ's face applies just as well to interpreting scripture: "Rather than fashioning the Lord [or the scriptures] in my own image, I must be refashioned in his [or theirs]. To see [the scriptures], I must come to have [their] image in my countenance. I must come to see everything and everyone the way [they] see me."

In the end, we haven't landed far apart. The vision of Christ in section 110 worked on both of us to provoke desire for an unhindered, material relationship with Christ. For all the vision's spectacular symbolic imagery, it moved our thoughts in tandem, if on different conceptual paths, toward lived and tangible covenant relationship. It led both of us to the place where the veil is lifted from the mind of the Bride and the face of the Bridegroom is seen in its beloved specificity. To the place where eternity is pressure injected into time.

> The Lord bless [you], and keep [you]:
> The Lord make his face to shine upon [you], and be gracious unto [you]:
> The Lord lift up his countenance upon [you], and give [you] peace. (Numbers 6:24–26)

Rosalynde

— CHAPTER 6 —

Christ as He Is

DOCTRINE AND COVENANTS 130

This revelation consists of several items of instruction given by Joseph Smith. The Prophet teaches that the Father and Son may appear personally to human beings and that when the Savior shall appear, we will see that he is human like ourselves. Furthermore, the Prophet teaches that the reckoning of time is relative to one's position in the divine cosmos. Past, present, and future are continually before the Lord. In its sanctified state, the earth will become an instrument of revelation, and all inhabitants will be given revelatory knowledge of the higher kingdoms.

Joseph prophesies that the Civil War will begin in South Carolina and comments on the timing of the Second Coming. Knowledge and intelligence rise with us in the Resurrection. Blessings are predicated on a heavenly law. The Father and Son have tangible bodies of flesh and bone, but the Holy Ghost is a personage of Spirit.

> **"That same sociality which exists among us here will exist among us there." (Doctrine and Covenants 130:2)**

Rosalynde,

The form of section 130 belies, I think, its potential importance.

Rather than being presented in the voice of the Lord, dictated in the divine first person like section 19; or as a fourth-wall breaking vision that, like section 76, opens the heavens and bounds across space-time, section 130 presents itself as a modest assortment of loosely connected notes extracted from a pair of impromptu sermons given by Joseph Smith on April 2, 1843. It's a good example, maybe, of the divine "domesticity" that finally follows the longed-for marriage of Christ and Church.

In this way, section 130 seems, at first glance, to be a grab bag of teachings, a potpourri of doctrines, that, apart from their shared occasion, have nothing in particular in common. Some of this section's claims about God's embodiment, terse as they are, are more clearly taught here than anywhere else, and it's obvious why we'd want them canonized in our scriptures. But some of its other teachings—for example, about how angels "reside in the presence of God, on a globe like a sea of glass and fire" (130:7)—seem to float free of the rest and resist easy interpretation.

This modest, miscellaneous quality, though, is one of the things I like about section 130. This section reads like a collection of orphaned footnotes. It has the look of something secretarial. It has the feel of something scrawled hastily on the back of an envelope when William Clayton, patting his pockets in search of a pen, decided he'd really better be writing some of this stuff down.

In exactly this way, section 130 is "like unto [a] treasure hid" in an open field (Matthew 13:44).

The section's humble and abbreviated form masks a series of potent revelations that have enormous scope and far-reaching consequences. And it seems to me, these fragments might actually best be understood as part of a coherent mosaic, as shards of a unified set of responses that cluster around the singular doctrine at the heart of Joseph's original sermon: the truly radical idea that the "same sociality which exists among us here will exist among us there" (130:2).

The story of this section goes like this: On Sunday, April 2, 1843, Joseph Smith presided over a stake conference in Ramus, Illinois. In the Sunday morning session, Orson Hyde spoke and took John 14:23 and 1 John 3:2 as his texts. Both texts address what it would mean to be visited by God and, thus, to "see him as he is" (1 John 3:2). At lunch, Joseph told Orson that, when the conference reconvened, he wanted to offer some corrections to that morning's sermon. Orson was grateful. Joseph then gave a pair of sermons and, over the course of his remarks, offered both the promised corrections and some additional comments on the nature of time. William Clayton took notes, and Willard Richards copied these notes into Joseph's journal. From there, historian Steven Harper explains, "Some of the teachings were clarified and prepared for publication in the Church's newspaper in the 1850s and then added to the 1876 edition of the Doctrine and Covenants, becoming Section 130."[25]

What, then, do John 14:23 and 1 John 3:2 say? And what, especially, did Joseph add by way of clarification?

In John 14:23, Jesus teaches that "if a man love me, he will keep my words: and my Father will love him, and we will come unto him, and make our abode with him."

In 1 John 3:2, John teaches: "Beloved, now we are the sons of God, and it doth not yet appear what we shall be: but we know that, when he shall appear, we shall be like him; for we shall see him as he is."

The heart of Joseph's clarification is given in the very first verse of section 130. He starts from the text of 1 John 3:2 and then adds one unassuming line. "When the Savior shall appear we shall see him as he is. We shall see that he is a man like ourselves" (130:1).

What will we see when we see him?

We will see "a man like ourselves."

Verse 22 then doubles down on this claim by extending it to include both the Father and the Son: "The Father has a body of flesh and bones as tangible as man's; the Son also; but the Holy Ghost has not a body of flesh and bones, but is a personage of Spirit. Were it not so, the Holy Ghost could not dwell in us" (130:22).

What will we see when we see either the Father or the Son?

Someone with "a body of flesh and bones as tangible as man's."

We will see, as Joseph memorably teaches almost exactly a year later, that "God himself, who sits enthroned in yonder heavens, is a man like unto one of yourselves, that is the great secret. If the vail was rent to-day, and the great God, who holds this world in its orbit, and upholds all things by his power; if you were to see him to-day, you would see him in all the person, image and very form as a man."[26]

As simple as it sounds, this is a bold and—from the perspective of the broader Christian tradition—utterly heretical teaching. Given traditional ideas about God's true nature, Joseph has gone so far off the rails with this claim that his position skirts atheism.

Sure, it's broadly accepted among Christians that God, in the historical person of Jesus, condescended to incarnate himself as a human being for the sake of our redemption—but God is not, in his divine essence, anything like a human being. God the Father not only doesn't have a body but also wholly transcends anything created, temporal, or material. And while the idea that Jesus, as God incarnate, must somehow be both fully human and fully divine is foundational to all the traditional creeds, this union of humanity and divinity in the person of Jesus is, nonetheless, treated by the tradition as both the biggest scandal and the greatest mystery in the universe. God and humans are so different that their miraculous unity in Jesus, despite its reality, remains the picture of absurdity.

Joseph, though, isn't worried about any of this.

Ignoring the creeds, he trusts what God has revealed to him. And when Orson Hyde preaches on 1 John 3:2 and still sounds a little too like other creeds, Joseph doesn't hesitate to revisit those same themes and offer, by way of correction and clarification, what he's learned.

When we see him, "we shall see," Joseph simply says, "that he is a man like ourselves" (130:1).

This point, though, isn't just scholastic. This isn't ivory-tower shadowboxing. For Joseph, this point couldn't be more practical. And from his point of view, it's tied directly to our most immediate practical concerns: our concerns about how to be saved, about how to enter into a real relationship with God, about how to live in such a way that the Father and Son will come to us and make their abode with us (see John 14:23).

What's at stake here is the nature of salvation itself. Or as Doctrine and Covenants 130:2 puts it, the deeply practical question in play here concerns the nature of divine "sociality."

What Joseph seems keen to deny is that divine sociality is, at root, anything other than a fully material and fully embodied form of sociality.

Because God "has a body of flesh and bones as tangible as man's," we can count on the fact that the "same sociality which exists among us here will exist among us there" (130:22, 2). We can count on the fact that, as verse three clarifies with respect to John 14:23, "the appearing of the Father and the Son, in that verse, is a personal appearance; and the idea that the Father and the Son dwell in a man's heart is an old sectarian notion, and is false" (131:3).

Now, as you noted earlier, divine "indwelling"—as taught in section 76 and, especially, by Jesus in John 14–17—is certainly a real and pivotal aspect of our redemption. As Jesus explains it, his disciples must, for the sake of their salvation, "all be one; as thou, Father, art in me, and I in thee, that they also may be one in us . . . I in them, and thou in me, that they may be made perfect in one" (John 17:21, 23).

To be saved, we must be made perfect "in" one: the Father in Christ and Christ in us, that we may also be one in them.

This is at-one-ment.

But the nature of this fully embodied form of divine indwelling—of this divine "sociality"—isn't immediately obvious. If we're now trying to think about indwelling and sociality in terms of bodies rather than immaterial spirits, then the goalposts have been moved a pretty dramatic distance. And to understand what's involved in an embodied form of indwelling, we may have to rethink a whole array of received ideas about God and salvation. We can't just borrow traditional models from our Christian brothers and sisters, models that view this indwelling as a purely "spiritual"—and, thus, unembodied—dwelling of the Father and Son "in a man's heart" (130:3).

In fact, while Doctrine and Covenants 130:22 does allow for the Holy Ghost to be "a personage of Spirit," rather than a personage of flesh and bone, so that it can "dwell in us," Doctrine and Covenants 131 goes on to rule out every attempt to think about *anything*, including "spirit," as something other than a form of matter: "There is no such thing as immaterial matter. All spirit is matter, but it is more fine or pure, and can only be discerned by purer eyes; we cannot see it; but when our bodies are purified we shall see that it is all matter" (131:7–8).

Yes, spirit isn't flesh and bone. But even as a personage of spirit, section 131 claims, the Holy Ghost is material. All spirit is matter, and a spirit body is still a material body.

Where, then, does this leave us?

I'm not sure. But I think it leaves us—that is, *all* of us—with a very specific job.

To make sense of what it might mean to finally "dwell in one" with an embodied Father and Son, we need to make sense (as Joseph originally indicated in verse two of section 130) of what it means to say that the same sociality which exists among us here will also exist among us there.

What is our "sociality" like *here*? And what aspects of this "sociality" will carry over *there*?

This is, as best I can tell, a truly knotty question.

To untangle it, we'd likely need answers to at least two other questions—patently philosophical questions—answers that we may not currently have. First, we'd need a working theory of what matter even is. And second, we'd need a better idea of how deeply materiality is intertwined with temporality. We'd need to know whether the connection between matter and time goes all the way down.

What is matter? And can matter be separated from time?

I'm not going to answer these big questions in the next couple of pages, but I think we might at least sharpen their edges by reflecting on what sociality *is* like in this world.

In this world, *sociality* is something like a name for our embodied relationships. And when section 130 promises that this world's sociality can continue beyond this life, it seems to be promising, in particular, that our most important family relationships can continue in the world to come. In this respect, family relationships may be a good model for divine sociality in general.

So, say we took marriage as a case study, as you've already encouraged us to do. What ingredients are needed for this kind of sociality to exist in the first place? And what is needed for this kind of relationship to persist and succeed?

It seems to me that one core ingredient for any kind of relationship is just this: a relationship must involve interactions. That is, in order for a relationship to exist, there must literally be *inter*-actions: actions that pass between us, actions that circulate, actions that we share.

For a relationship to exist, there must be give and take. There must be both giving and receiving, asking and answering, offering and accepting, claiming and recompensing. We must touch and be touched. We must need and be needed. We must choose and be chosen.

Grace for grace.

And these interactions must leave a mark. Who we are and what we do must matter to the other person. Our interactions must change them, and they, in turn, must change us.

In other words, for a marriage to be real, these interactions must also be real. And these interactions must have real stakes, real costs, and real consequences.

Choices, actions, and consequences are the stuff out of which marriages are made. They are the threads that weave lives together. They make sociality, as we know it, possible.

Or to put this another way, borrowing from the Church's legendary ad campaign, we might just say: "Family . . . isn't it about time?"

Sociality: isn't it about time?

In this world, all relationships—that is, sociality itself—are about time. They're made of time. They require time. Only time's persistent flow can make actions and consequences, and thus marriages and families, real and possible.

Sociality is the circulation, in time, of action and consequence.

Which brings me, finally, to the second half of verse two, the half that (suspiciously) I haven't yet quoted.

Yes, Joseph plainly teaches that the "same sociality which exists among us here will exist among us there." But he also adds this important qualification: "only it will be coupled with eternal glory, which glory we do not now enjoy" (130:2).

What could it mean to "couple" this kind of sociality—a sociality that is currently made of time and woven from interactions in time—with "eternal glory"?

If we weren't worried about matter and bodies, the answer would be simple. We would, again, just plug in a whole battery of assumptions borrowed from the broader Christian tradition, assumptions that treat God as unembodied and immaterial, and then we would read coupling something with eternal glory as simply liberating it from time. "Eternal glory" would name our successful and wholesale *escape* from time. And in the process, it would name our successful and wholesale escape not only from loss and suffering but also from the burden of action and consequence.

On that traditional view, eternal glory would save us from all of the trouble and vulnerability that living in time, performing actions, and suffering consequences seems to require. It would save us, in essence, from needing to exercise moral agency.

But if this is true, then I don't know what sense it would make to say that the *same* sociality we have here will also exist there. Sociality here is made of time. And a sociality that's been frozen in place by the addition of an unchanging "eternal glory"—i.e., a sociality without any ongoing progression, relations, interactions, or consequences—wouldn't be anything like the sort of sociality we have here.

In this respect, then, I don't think it's any accident that after verse two, the next nineteen verses all address the question of time.

Verse four, for example, seems to teach that God, with his body of flesh and bones, *does* exist in time. His time may be different from our time, but there is such a thing as what Joseph calls "God's time" (130:4). "In answer to the question—Is not the reckoning of God's time, angel's time, prophet's time, and man's time, according to the planet on which they reside? I answer, Yes" (130:4–5).

According to verse four, temporality is real but relative. Time passes for God, angels, and humans, but depending on *where* you are, time may pass differently for you.

But then verse 7 seems to walk back the idea of "God's time" and appears to suggest, instead, that God is in some way outside of time: "The angels do not reside on a planet like this earth; but they reside in the presence of God, on a globe like a sea of glass and fire, where all things for their glory are manifest, past, present, and future, and are continually before the Lord" (130:6–7). According to at least one common reading of this verse, past and present and future appear to be compounded for God. They are all—and all at once—continually before the Lord. Which is very interesting. But would also seem to imply a time-free mode of existence (and, thus, a time-independent form of sociality?) for God that is nothing like what we have here.

We might, though, try to weigh our readings of verses 4 and 7 against verses 20 and 21. And these verses may be both the most famous and the most decisive in this entire collection of loosely bound notes.

These often-quoted verses teach the following: "There is a law, irrevocably decreed in heaven before the foundations of this world, upon which all blessings are predicated—and when we obtain any blessing from God, it is by obedience to that law upon which it is predicated" (130:20–21).

To my ear, these verses seem to be a ringing and unqualified endorsement of the perpetual and irrevocable reality of actions and consequences.

There is a law that structures reality, our wholly material reality, and this law predicates consequences on actions. It predicates effects on causes. And if you have not performed the action, if you have not obeyed the law, then the blessed consequences of that action will not follow.

This law, it appears, can't be rolled back. It doesn't have any exceptions, loopholes, or escape clauses. It's irrevocable.

And again, as with sociality, I don't have the faintest idea what this law would mean without the ongoing reality of time, action, and consequence.

For this same reason, Joseph says, "If a person gains more knowledge and intelligence in this life through his diligence and obedience than another, he will have so much the advantage in the world to come" (130:19). Especially in this example, it seems clear that in the world to come, the reality of actions and consequences—and, thus, of time—is in some sense preserved. Otherwise, the "advantage" of having already gained intelligence through our relationships with God, loved ones, and the world at large wouldn't be preserved and wouldn't continue.

What might it mean, then, to couple this world's sociality with eternal glory? What might it mean if eternal glory is not an escape from time-bound bodies, actions, and consequences?

Our initial discussion of eternity in the context of Doctrine and Covenants 19 might be useful here. Section 19 took the notion of eternity quite seriously but also offered an unusual perspective that did not treat eternity as an escape from time or as an endless quantity of time. Rather, section 19 invited us to think about eternity as a divine dimension *of* time, a qualitatively divine way of handling time that blesses and redeems time, even as time continues to flow.

And helpfully enough, I think section 130 also includes an excellent example of this way of handling time—of "coupling" eternity *with* all the troubles and blessings of time.

On that same Sunday in 1843, Steven Harper reminds us, Joseph also addressed the prophecies of a contemporary preacher "named

William Miller, who had predicted that the Savior's second coming would be April 3, 1843, the day after conference."[27] In response to this provocative prediction, Joseph shared what *he* was told when he asked God about the timing of the Second Coming:

> I was once praying very earnestly to know the time of the coming of the Son of Man, when I heard a voice repeat the following: Joseph, my son, if thou livest until thou art eighty-five years old, thou shalt see the face of the Son of Man; therefore let this suffice, and trouble me no more on this matter. I was left thus, without being able to decide whether this coming referred to the beginning of the millennium or to some previous appearing, or whether I should die and thus see his face. I believe the coming of the Son of Man will not be any sooner than that time. (130:14–17)

In response to this question about when Christ would finally return, Joseph was told that, if he lived until the age of eighty-five, he would see the face of the Son of Man. And then he was told to accept this answer, let it go, and stop asking that question.

The trouble, of course, is that Joseph didn't know what this answer meant. He "was left thus, without being able to decide" whether this answer meant that Christ's second coming would happen when he was eighty-five or that Christ would appear to *him* for some other reason at the age of eighty-five or just that he would "see his face" when he was eighty-five because he would already be dead (130:16). On any of these readings, however, Joseph concluded that the Millennium probably wouldn't happen before that time.

How might this example help?

In her October 2023 general conference talk, Sister Amy A. Wright told a strikingly similar story about a poignant and powerful prayer she offered when she was first diagnosed with cancer:

In my mind I asked Heavenly Father, "Am I going to die?"

The Holy Ghost whispered, "Everything is going to be OK."

Then I asked, "Am I going to live?"

Again, the answer came: "Everything is going to be OK."[28]

To me, these prayers both seem to follow the same pattern. A difficult question about time is asked, specifically: how much time is left? And in both cases, God seems to reply: "Good question. Here, rather than a clear and final answer, is a blessing in response."

Perhaps this offers a rough sketch for how eternity might join hands with time, for how eternal glory might couple with an embodied sociality, for how grace might intervene and still preserve both action and consequence.

Does it matter when Christ will come again? Yes, absolutely.

Does it matter if we live or die? Yes, absolutely.

But regardless of when Christ returns—regardless of whether I die tomorrow or live until I'm eighty-five—will it be okay?

Yes, "everything is going to be OK."

Here, eternal glory doesn't stop time or supplant time or allow us to escape time. Rather, eternity shelters and blesses it.

Adam

> "They reside in the presence of God, on a globe like a sea of glass and fire, where all things for their glory are manifest, past, present, and future, and are continually before the Lord." (Doctrine and Covenants 130:7)

Adam,

We had apple pie for dessert the other night, and my father-in-law served it in a way I'd never seen. The pie was baked in a rectangular casserole dish, not a pie plate, so instead of cutting wedges he just scooped out a big steaming spoonful of crust and apple. I asked him instead to scrape the sides of the dish to gather up a serving of the crunchy baked-on remnants at the edge. I'd choose those crumbly, crispy bits any day over the soft center. As I recall, you're not a pie guy yourself. Maybe you'd choose the same?

I'm reminded of those buttery crumbs because of your description of section 130's "modest, miscellaneous" form—its composition from six or so separate thoughts, noted without much context or development but loosely connected around the idea of encountering Christ. Section 130 looks and tastes different from the mega-revelations—those heaping scoops of scriptural language—in sections 76 and 88. I like these crunchy little edge pieces.

The sundriness of its form mirrors the fragmentary, incremental, inspired human process that led to the canonized text we have today. You pointed out a bit of that textual history, and I think it helpfully illuminates what we've been calling *revelation* in these letters. As you note, this section originated as Joseph's spoken "corrections" to a sermon by Orson Hyde. Sometime between 1843 and 1846, Willard Richards recorded these teachings in Joseph's journal, likely relying on William Clayton's contemporaneous diary. About ten years later, in Utah, the Clayton and Richards records were integrated and inscribed by hand into what's now called the Manuscript History of the Church, under the direction of George A. Smith, a member of the First Presidency, and overseen by Brigham Young. The existing manuscript shows clear traces of several substantive revisions, including the addition of the phrase "were it not so the Holy Ghost could not dwell in us."

These Church leaders and their scribes worked to make sense of the role of the Holy Ghost in light of the materiality of its spirit personage, while remaining in harmony with the records before them. In 1856, this modified text appeared in print form in the *Deseret News*—remember, these writings were not yet considered scripture—with minor changes in punctuation and orthography introduced by the editor of the paper. It appeared in print again two years later in the Church newspaper *Millennial Star*, with additional changes in punctuation. It was this 1858 version that, under the direction of Orson Pratt, was added to the 1876 edition of the Doctrine and Covenants, a volume that was brought before the Saints and officially canonized on October 10, 1880, by a vote at a general conference of the Church.[29]

Fine-grained textual history like this isn't critically important for the kind of reading you and I are doing here, but it helps us understand what, as Latter-day Saints, we mean by revelation when we're talking about canonized scripture. We don't (can't, given the eighth Article of Faith's affirmation that "we believe the Bible to be the word of God as far as it is translated correctly") hold a view of revelation as a transparent transcription, error free and untouchable, of divine language as it originally issued from God's mouth. Multiple human minds and hands, working under the influence of the Holy Ghost, touched these "shards," as you called them, during the multistage process by which revelation became canonized scripture. Blessed be those minds and hands!

Do the human minds and social processes that aided in the transformation of Joseph's inspired shards into canonized scripture in any way diminish the legitimacy of section 130? No, not for Latter-day Saints, not when we rightly appreciate what scripture is and isn't. Because we have access to living prophets, we needn't rely on scripture to determine correct doctrine and policy for the present-day Church. Continuing revelation through inspired leaders makes those calls. Church leaders consult deeply the scriptures, of course, in making their inspired determinations of doctrine. Scripture matters. But the ultimate authority is direct, Spirit-mediated revelation. And because we, as rank-and-file readers of scripture, have access to personal revelation, we needn't rely solely on the text of scripture to somehow determine our daily decisions.

Scripture can and should act as a medium for prophetic and personal revelation—we've seen that process up close in several of these visions—but it shouldn't be mistaken for final doctrinal or personal authority. As President Jeffrey R. Holland taught, "The scriptures are not the ultimate source of knowledge for Latter-day Saints. They are manifestations of the ultimate source. The ultimate source of knowledge and authority for a Latter-day Saint is the living God. The communication of those gifts comes from God as living, vibrant, divine revelation."[30]

This is great news for scripture lovers like you and me, I think. Scripture is freed up to be for readers what it is best suited to be: a place to build a personal relationship with God. This does not mean that its interpretation is endlessly flexible or that we project our own wished-for meanings onto its surface. On the contrary, we come to scripture to be remade in light of the images of Christ we find in them. If scripture is a partial record of the human family's Spirit-aided experiences with God, then it makes sense to read scripture to seek our own Spirit-aided experiences with God, experiences like the one Joseph and Sidney received together as they studied John 5:29: "By the power of the Spirit our eyes were opened and our understandings were enlightened, so as to see and understand the things of God" (Doctrine and Covenants 76:12). The effect of such an experience, as I understand it, is not just intellectual but existential: as a reader, I'm transformed by the divine light that meets me in the arena of scripture.

And if, as we saw with Joseph and Sidney, these encounters occur as we prayerfully search, interpret, question, translate, analyze, liken, ponder, and discuss the text, then anything that draws our attention more deeply into its words—its human and historical dimensions or its linguistic difficulty or formal oddities, as in section 130—serves the ultimate aim of keeping us engaged in our encounter with divine light.

It's quite possible that a clearly explained, transparently sourced, systematic version of these teachings, if we can imagine such a thing, would actually be *less* engaging as scripture—that is, as a place to seek Spirit-aided experiences with divinity. The purpose of canonization, under this model, is not to guarantee a text's doctrinal inerrancy, because scripture is not inerrant. Instead, to designate an inspired text as "canonized scripture" is to set it apart as a holy place in which to share our lives with God and to make it available as common ground for shared exploration with our fellow Saints, a project that has the side effect of bonding us as a people.

All this is just what you and I have been trying to model in this book. And all this is just what I've experienced—the searching, the meeting, and the bonding.

In that spirit of sharing, I'll admit something embarrassing. I've quoted Doctrine and Covenants 130:2 many times to make the point that our eternal relationships will be of the same kind, and embedded in the same sacred network, as our sealed earthly relationships: "And that same sociality which exists among us here will exist among us there, only it will be coupled with eternal glory, which glory we do not now enjoy." I treasure that teaching, and I believe it. But all these years I think I've missed the most important, very obvious, point of that verse: Christ is included in that circle of sociality both here and there! In other words, "That same sociality [including myself, my associates, and the Savior] which exists among us here will exist among us there." The quality of relationship that I am willing to share with Christ in this life, here and now—my "sociality" with Christ in the present—is essentially the same quality that defines eternal life in his presence. Whatever intensity or fulness is added by the coupling of eternal glory, it doesn't radically change the fundamental basis of the relationship.

In this new light, section 130 seems to me to show with special clarity the urgent prophetic commission that fell to Joseph in the last years of his ministry: namely, to lead his people to the "same sociality" with God that had sustained him from one moment to another throughout his life. As a prophet, Joseph was acquainted early with divine beings: as a seer, he looked into the oracular depths of his Urim and Thummim and sensed knowledge flowing by divine power; as a revelator, he allowed the veil to fall from his eyes and saw the Lord standing before him in glorious body. The almost casual familiarity with which Joseph alludes to "the same sociality [with Jesus Christ] which exists among us here" (130:2) points, I think, to the perceptible, interrelational quality of the Prophet's presence with Christ.

Joseph created a genuinely shared life with God. How is this life in Christ multiplied and distributed to everybody?

Was Joseph's perceptible, interrelational union different in kind or in degree from the enlargement and enlightenment that sometimes comes upon me when I'm in the scriptures? Am I anywhere in the neighborhood of "that same sociality"?

This is not a theoretical question. The Lord promises his divine presence to all, as Brother Orson had, however clumsily, pointed out in his March 1843 sermon to which Joseph responded with his "corrections." Orson had quoted John 14:23: "Jesus answered and said unto him, If a man love me, he will keep my words: and my Father will love him, and we will come unto him, and make our abode with him." But how was this to happen? Perhaps it was less mysterious than previously thought!

Section 130 teaches that divine beings are perceptible bodies "as tangible as man's" (130:22). And as for the Urim and Thummim, an individual stone will be "given to each of those who come into the celestial kingdom" (130:11). Even at the height of its ethereal, esoteric imagery, section 130 is really about the practical project of democratically distributing the means of revelation—the means to share one's life with God—to all who will receive it. The generosity of that project originates in the character of the God in whose life Joseph shared: "This is my work and my glory, to bring to pass the immortality and eternal life of man" (Moses 1:39).

I'm grateful for this generous impulse to distribute revelation as widely as possible. Visions of Christ are potent, sometimes unpredictable religious motivators. Claimed visionary experiences can be the kernel of apostasy, even violence, especially when they are wielded in ways designed to elevate the visionary as a spiritual celebrity and isolate his or her followers. What I see in the vision of Christ promised in section 130, though, is the opposite. They aren't meant to foster spiritual exclusivity. They aren't just for the benefit of the favored few with the secret knowledge. Emphatically to the contrary, they beg to be understood in the context of section 76's expansive salvation theology, section 45's open-door-policy Zion, and section 88's *already* and *not yet*. In this light, section 130 shows us a renewed world in which the entire planet will become a revelatory instrument to broadcast the knowledge and the glory of God to all who will receive it. What God could be more prodigal with his presence?

This leads me to my final point. I wonder if God's generosity might also shed light on the question of time and timelessness that you lay out so well, Adam. I'm with you: both reason and personal experience suggest that the vision of eternal life drawn in this section—eternal life as our continued material association with one another and with the material God in whose image we are made—requires the flow of time. Without time there's no possibility of change, and without change there's no possibility for genuine relationships that are at the heart of the Restoration's doctrine of salvation: relationships of mutual giving and receiving that change us over and over again.

So if eternity is not our liberation from time but the "qualitatively divine way of handling time that blesses and redeems," as you suggest, then what is the quality with which God handles time? And what are we to make of the evocative language in this section that, as you noted, seems to suggest a kind of divine timelessness? "All things . . . are manifest, past, present, and future, and are continually before the Lord" (130:7).

I have an idea, and I wonder what you think about it. I think that God's characteristic trait in handling time is generosity, or grace—the same generosity that motivates this section's aim to distribute the means of revelation so widely.

Here's my hypothesis: in section 130, the Lord gently makes his point about handling time with generosity by drawing on the scriptural imagery of apocalypse. Every book of scripture contains apocalyptic visions—passages of narrative and imagery that tell of the ultimate coming of Christ to dwell on earth, his winning over of evil, his righteous judgment, and the full establishment of the kingdom of God. Apocalyptic prophecies have a time-arrow built in: they highlight the role of time as a stage for the unfolding of sacred history. They point in one direction only, propelling time forward toward its future wrapping-up. The book of Revelation, which has been such an important partner-text in our explorations here, is the classic example of apocalyptic prophecy. And, as we've seen, its imagery is everywhere in section 130.

Apocalyptic prophecy represents the "not yet" futurity of the "already and not yet" promise I explored in section 88. And as I said there, I place faith in the promise that Christ will come to establish his kingdom of love, and I'm grateful to be part of a people whose vibrant faith is fired, in part, by these promises.

But apocalyptic prophecy is easily hijacked for fantasies of grievance and retribution. It's incredibly tempting to imagine that the establishment of God's kingdom will mean the settling of scores. Christ will finally sweep down from heaven to punish my enemies and mete out the vengeance that has been so long delayed! This way of thinking shackles time, and its relentless movement forward, to personal projects of revenge and retaliation.

As we've seen again and again in these visions of Christ and the kingdom he brings, the Restoration's unique vision of salvation is incompatible with this kind of vengeful hijacking of apocalyptic prophecy. Christ unlocks both the gates of Zion and the gates of hell and generously invites each to receive the glory that he or she is willing to abide. Human vengeance and retaliation, and divine retributive violence, are categorically ruled out. Time no longer rushes relentlessly toward an ultimate settling of scores. The arrow of vengeance is taken out of the flow of time.

So here, in a nutshell, is my tentative reading of the seeming erasure of time in section 130: the timeless quality of existence in the presence of God is about abandoning the apocalyptic arrow of time. When we receive the fulness of God's generous presence, we enter a place where time is no longer shackled to projects of punishment and vindication. Instead, time is graciously freed. Freed for genuine, embodied relationship—"that same sociality"—with Christ, with one another, and with the present unfolding of God's generous, gracious work of salvation.

Rosalynde

— CHAPTER 7 —

Christ the Liberator

DOCTRINE AND COVENANTS 138

In this revelation, President Joseph F. Smith ponders the first epistle of Peter, the atonement of Jesus Christ, and his visit to the spirits in the spirit world after his crucifixion. President Smith receives a vision of the spirit world filled with an innumerable company of the dead. He sees the righteous, who are filled with joy and happiness. They anticipate the coming of Christ to the spirit world and look forward to their resurrection and liberation from the bondage of death.

The prophet observes the Savior's coming and his preaching of the gospel to this company of the dead. Christ commissions them to carry the glad tidings to the disobedient spirits so that all the dead, small and great, may learn of him. President Smith sees many of God's mightiest sons and daughters engaged in this ministry, prepared from the premortal existence for this work. He sees that the righteous dead of the latter days may also join this postmortal ministry.

Rosalynde,

This is a formulation I will definitely remember: rather than liberating us from time, Christ liberates time itself. He sets time free. He frees it from the burden of satisfying our desires and settling our scores. He frees it from the shackles of vanity and vengeance.

Eternity is time liberated.

Well said.

With section 138 we come to the end of both the Doctrine and Covenants and the seven visions of Christ we planned to consider. And so it's fitting that this vision is itself concerned, above all, with life's end.

Section 138 is about death. It's about what happens to our dead—where they go, what they do, and what they hope for.

And most astonishing of all, this revelation is about Christ's own experience of death. Rather than offering a vision of the pre-mortal Christ, the mortal Christ, or even the resurrected Christ, President Joseph F. Smith's singular vision shows us a Christ who is *himself* dead, a Christ who has joined the dead in death, if only for three days, in order to personally "declare their redemption from the bands of death" (138:16).

Section 138 presents a restored vision of what Christians once called Christ's "harrowing of hell," and, in doing so, it draws back death's curtain to reveal what happened after "God himself" became "subject even unto death, the will of the Son being swallowed up in the will of the Father" (Mosiah 15:1, 7).

This vision was given to President Smith on October 3, 1918, less than two months before his own passing, and with it we make a huge historical leap, out of the early nineteenth century and into the teeth of the twentieth. If I can be forgiven for drawing one last time on our friend Steven Harper's valuable historical work, I'll let him set the dark scene: "Death haunted mankind in 1918. The Great War, known today as World War I, was in the process of claiming more than nine million lives. That staggering figure paled in comparison with the number of people slain in even less time by a global influenza pandemic. Worldwide the virus reaped a grim harvest of perhaps fifty million souls. It killed more than 195,000 Americans in October 1918, the deadliest month in American history, the month the Lord revealed Doctrine and Covenants 138."[31]

This is the black night out of which section 138's bright light shines.

President Smith received the vision on October 3, and the very next day, on October 4, he shared it with the world in his opening address at general conference.

"I sat in my room pondering over the scriptures," he said, "reflecting upon the great atoning sacrifice that was made by the Son of God, for the redemption of the world" (138:1–2). While pondering, his mind was drawn to Peter's account of how Christ was "put to death in the flesh" and "went and preached unto the spirits in prison" (1 Peter 3:18, 19). In this way, Peter taught, "was the gospel preached also to them that are dead, that they might be judged according to men in the flesh, but live according to God in the spirit" (1 Peter 4:6).

These verses occasioned the vision that followed.

"The eyes of my understanding were opened," President Smith said, "and I saw the hosts of the dead, both small and great," including "an innumerable company of the spirits of the just, who had been faithful in the testimony of Jesus while they lived in mortality" (138:11, 12).

This vision, though, wasn't contemporaneous. Instead, it was showing him something that had already happened, almost two thousand years before.

This innumerable company of the just had all "gathered together in one place" in anticipation of something (138:12). Or better, they were all gathered together to wait for *someone*: "They were assembled awaiting the advent of the Son of God into the spirit world, to declare their redemption from the bands of death" (138:16).

While Christ's mortal disciples passed an excruciating night, destroyed by their Master's death, unsure of what would happen next, "this vast multitude waited and conversed, rejoicing in the hour of their deliverance from the chains of death" (138:18). And as they rejoiced, "the Son of God appeared, declaring liberty to the captives" and "preached to them the everlasting gospel" (138:18, 19).

In response, the faithful host bowed before him; "their countenances shone, and the radiance from the presence of the Lord rested upon them, and they sang praises unto his holy name" (138:24).

The image of Christ displayed in this vision is not of Christ as a suffering servant, as an enthroned king, or as a son returned to the bosom of his father. The image of Christ displayed in this vision is of Christ as liberator, as rescuer, as one holding that fistful of keys needed to deliver the captives from bondage and wrench open death's stubborn prison doors.

In this vision, perhaps more clearly than anywhere else, we see Christ fulfilling that Isaianic prophecy with which he publicly announced his mortal ministry: "The Spirit of the Lord is upon me, because he hath anointed me to preach the gospel to the poor; he hath sent me to heal the brokenhearted, to preach deliverance to the captives, and recovering of sight to the blind, to set at liberty them that are bruised" (Luke 4:18; see also Isaiah 61:1).

Beyond this striking image, President Smith's vision also has, I think, an unusual structure. President Smith's vision of Christ is not one like Joseph and Oliver's vision in section 110, where Christ appears personally, in the present tense. Instead, President Smith has a vision of Christ appearing in the past to someone else. He gets to peek over someone else's shoulder. He witnesses an innumerable company of the dead who in turn witness the appearance of Christ.

President Smith witnesses the dead who witness Christ.

And in this sense, he has—appropriately enough—what we might call a "vicarious" vision of Christ that, rather than being routed directly and immediately through his own person, is routed indirectly, and with a two-thousand-year delay, through a vast multitude of others.

President Smith's own description of the vision bears this out. His descriptions focus primarily on the visited dead rather than the visiting Christ.

While two verses are dedicated to narrating Christ's appearance (see 138:18–19), the section spends seven verses describing the gathered multitude while they wait for this appearance (see 138:11–17). Then, arguably, the bulk of the remaining forty or so verses describe who was there and what that faithful multitude did after Christ visited them.

This is a vision of Christ, but it's a vision of Christ wrapped inside a much broader and deeper vision of the "hosts of the dead" (138:11).

Similarly, rather than describing how Christ looked when he appeared, President Smith describes how the dead looked when *they* saw him appear: "their countenances shone, and the radiance from the presence of the Lord rested upon them" (138:24). While Joseph and Oliver describe in Doctrine and Covenants 110:3 how the Lord's "countenance shone above the brightness of the sun," President Smith describes how that brightness was reflected, vicariously, in the faces of those who witnessed it. He describes how the dead, upon seeing Christ, bore his image in their countenances (see Alma 5:14).

We see Christ's glory but only in *their* eyes.

This same oblique angle of approach is evident in the vision's most original doctrinal contribution: President Smith's revelation that when Christ visited the dead, he only visited the faithful who had assembled to greet him. He didn't personally visit those who weren't already waiting for him.

"The Lord went not in person among the wicked and the disobedient who had rejected the truth, to teach them," in part because "his ministry among those who were dead was limited to the brief time intervening between the crucifixion and his resurrection" (138:29, 27). So, instead, Christ devoted his brief visit to commissioning the faithful to teach and love on his behalf, endowing them with his power so that they could represent him to the remainder of the dead. "Behold, from among the righteous, he organized his forces and appointed messengers, clothed with power and authority, and commissioned them to go forth and carry the light of the gospel to them that were in darkness" (138:30).

However, this vicarious ministry, conducted in the name of the Lord, only gets us halfway there.

To close the loop and bring the remaining dead into the presence of God, they must accept the same gospel as the living, including "faith in God, repentance from sin, vicarious baptism for the remission of sins, the gift of the Holy Ghost by the laying on of hands, and all other principles of the gospel that were necessary" (138:33–34). The only twist is that, unlike the living, the dead are taught "*vicarious* baptism for the remission of sins" (emphasis added).

To be saved, the dead must accept a message delivered by those who minister vicariously in Christ's name and on his behalf. And to seal their acceptance, the living must also act vicariously in the name of the dead and on their behalf.

Christs suffers vicariously.

His ministers represent him vicariously.

And the believing dead must be baptized vicariously.

This is the vicarious round of love and service that braids one life into another. This is the vicarious round of interactions and consequences that seals lives and serves as a "welding link" between generations, because "they without us cannot be made perfect—neither can we without our dead be made perfect" (Doctrine and Covenants 128:18, 15). And this vicarious round is, I think, how divine "indwelling" is enacted and accomplished, with bodies standing in for bodies, and those bodies standing in for still other bodies, as names are exchanged and we all learn to act on behalf of one another.

"I in them, and thou in me," as Jesus said, "that they may be made perfect in one" (John 17:23).

This is what love and atonement look like. And only this vast, selfless, vicarious work—a vicarious work catalyzed by Christ's own vicarious sacrifice—can set in motion "a whole and complete and perfect union, and welding together of dispensations, and keys, and powers, and glories," a perfect union of all things "from the days of Adam even to the present time" (Doctrine and Covenants 128:18).

From the days of Adam even down to the present time! The ambition of this vicarious work is staggering.

And in his own vision, President Smith is drawn down this very same dispensational path. After describing how Christ's ministers are commissioned, President Smith proceeds to take attendance, calling roll and highlighting who, exactly, "among the great and mighty ones . . . were assembled in this vast congregation" (138:38). Among the members of this congregation, he names Adam, Eve, Abel, Seth, Noah, Shem, Abraham, Isaac, Jacob, Moses, Isaiah,

Ezekiel, Daniel, Elias, Malachi, and a catchall addendum—"even the prophets who dwelt among the Nephites" (138:49). And then, though they aren't counted among the "dead" per se, President Smith also names Joseph Smith Jr., Hyrum Smith (President Smith's own father), Brigham Young, John Taylor, and Wilford Woodruff as being among the spirits present for this occasion (see 138:53).

In this whole list, only one person—one critical person—is mentioned obliquely, indirectly, by way of someone else, rather than being named in his own right as a member of this congregation.

This one person is Elijah.

Rather than being named directly, Elijah is mentioned only in connection with Malachi:

> And Malachi, the prophet who testified of the coming of Elijah—of whom also Moroni spake to the Prophet Joseph Smith, declaring that he should come before the ushering in of the great and dreadful day of the Lord. . . . The Prophet Elijah was to plant in the hearts of the children the promises made to their fathers, foreshadowing the great work to be done in the temples of the Lord in the dispensation of the fulness of times, for the redemption of the dead, and the sealing of the children to their parents, lest the whole earth be smitten with a curse and utterly wasted at his coming. (138:46–48)

What better description of vicarious relationships—that is, of "indwelling"—could we get than this: that "the Prophet Elijah was to plant in the hearts of the children the promises made to their fathers" (138:47)?

It's interesting to me, though, that President Smith's paraphrase of Malachi 4:5–6 doesn't follow the letter of the Old Testament text. Rather, it follows the version of the text quoted to Joseph Smith by the angel Moroni in 1823 when, repeating his message four times, Moroni briefed Joseph on his future prophetic work.

As recorded in Doctrine and Covenants 2, Moroni's expanded variation on Malachi goes like this: "And he shall plant in the hearts of the children the promises made to the fathers, and the hearts of the children shall turn to their fathers. If it were not so, the whole earth would be utterly wasted at his coming" (2:2–3; see also Joseph Smith—History 1:29–50).

In comparison, Malachi's own shorter version goes like this: "And he shall turn the heart of the fathers to the children, and the heart of the children to their fathers, lest I come and smite the earth with a curse" (Malachi 4:6).

Moroni's variation intensifies the potential consequences of failure, from the earth being smitten with "a curse" to "the whole earth" being "utterly wasted." In addition, Malachi's version lacks entirely Moroni's beautiful image of the parents' promises being "planted" in the children's hearts.

Instead, Malachi's version uses the same verb in *both* halves of his prophecy, connecting parents to children in the same way children are connected to their parents. It's still a question of hearts, but in the case of both parents and children, their hearts are described as "turning."

This image of hearts turning is more subtle, but especially in Malachi's original Hebrew, it has the advantage of adding a powerful resonance that may be more difficult to hear in English.

For my part, I've always been struck by how in Hebrew the root word for "turning," *shuv,* is not only used in the physical sense to describe how someone might turn toward home (as in Genesis 31:3 where God tells Jacob to "return unto the land of thy fathers") but can also be used to describe a spiritual call to *repent* and turn back to God. For example, in Deuteronomy 30:2, Moses tells the Israelites that they will eventually "return [*shuv*] unto the Lord thy God, and shalt obey his voice according to all that I command thee this day." Or in Jeremiah 3:22, the Lord commands his people to "return [*shuv*], ye backsliding children, and I will heal your backslidings."

Moreover, the primary Hebrew word reserved for repentance is *teshuvah*, which is built from this same root, *shuv*.

Which is all just to say that, whenever I read Malachi 4:6 and hear Malachi talking about hearts "turning," I can't help but also hear him talking about repentance.

A heart that has "turned" is a heart that has "repented."

I don't think this connection is accidental or especially surprising. What other work, really, could possibly reunite the whole human family? What other kind of work but repentance could possibly heal all our broken families? What other kind of work could allow the whole human family, from Adam to the present day, to "be made perfect in one" by Christ's atonement (John 17:23)?

And if Jesus's own very clear and very compact formula for repentance is to be taken seriously, to successfully repent—i.e., to be forgiven—I must ultimately do one specific thing. To be forgiven, *I must forgive.*

"Forgive, and ye shall be forgiven" (Luke 6:37).

What then does it mean for the hearts of the fathers to turn to the children? I think it means, especially, that the fathers will forgive their children.

And what does it mean for the hearts of the children to turn to the fathers? I think it means, especially, that the children will forgive their fathers.

What form will this vast, intergenerational work of forgiveness take? It will take the form of a vicarious work. It will take the form of parents forgiving their children, of parents surrendering their own interests to act for and on behalf of their children. And it will take the form of children forgiving their parents, of children surrendering their own interests to act for and on behalf of their parents.

This, as you suggested, is how we liberate time. This is the "great work to be done," not only in our homes and hearts but also "in the temples of the Lord in the dispensation of the fulness of times, for the redemption of the dead, and the sealing of the children to their parents" (138:48).

"The dead who repent will be redeemed," President Smith concludes, and "thus was the vision of the redemption of the dead revealed to me" (138:58, 60).

Adam

"Their countenances shone, and the radiance from the presence of the Lord rested upon them, and they sang praises unto his holy name." (Doctrine and Covenants 138:24)

Adam,

My grandfather died last year at 103 years old. I wrote about him in *Seven Gospels*, when he was in the last months of his life. His work-torn hands and his long life as a servant-leader in a tiny farming community helped me think through the gospel of Benjamin, that iconic servant-leader who preached Christ with his last breaths.

A few days before Grandpa died, I went to visit him in the brick home he built on a country corner almost seven decades previously. He was lying on a hospital bed in the TV room, where Cougar football could keep him company. He looked still and shrunken under the sheet. I stood at his side, held his hands, and spoke to him. I wondered if he could hear me. Grandpa's hearing and vision had been poor for years, and I assumed that his mind had already entered the twilight passage between life and death. Still, I wanted to speak out loud how much I loved him and what his life had meant to me.

"Grandpa, you've been a noble servant your whole life. Nobody could have loved us and served us and taught us better than you did." I squeezed his hands and moved closer to his face. "Now you're being called to another mission."

His eyes flew open, and he lifted his head off the pillow. "I am?! Where to?"

In the tender comedy of the moment, I wanted to laugh and cry. His hoarse tone communicated both his absolute shock at receiving another mission assignment and his absolute willingness to serve. If I had handed him a white envelope from Salt Lake City, I have no doubt he'd have tried to get to his feet and find his shoes.

My grandfathers, both of them, were among those "faithful elders of this dispensation" (138:57). The years Grandpa spent confined to his recliner were, I think, the most trying "bondage" he endured (138:50). The life he loved was ten decades of consecrated "labor in [God's] vineyard" (138:56)—for him, an arid ribbon of valley tucked between the San Pitch Mountains and the Wasatch Plateau. The eternal life he sought was more of the same.

Your reading of section 138 tore the wrapper off this text for me. I love the way you split-screen the despairing huddle of the earthside disciples with the joyful anticipation of the dead gathered prisonside. You helped me see this passage as an Easter text: a fifth account of Christ's death to complement the accounts of the four New Testament evangelists. In separate witnesses transposed across the canon, Christ's living presence rises and sets over the horizon of death. On Thursday the disciples feasted in the presence of the Lord (see John 13), while the assembled spirits waited in darkness, imprisoned by their separation from God (see Doctrine and Covenants 138:11). But now an early Easter dawns on Holy Saturday: as the disciples mourn his absence, the assembled spirits rejoice in the glory of his coming. Christ goes from prison to prison—from the garden tomb to the spirits' bondage—and makes temples of them both.

I love how this section evokes an atmosphere of vibrating, electric anticipation among the assembly of the dead. Their joy is simply to be together, expecting God (see 138:12–18). We're told that the dead "[sing] praises unto his holy name" (138:24). I imagine their hymn is an Easter anthem:

He is risen! He is risen!
He hath opened heaven's gate.
We are free from sin's dark prison,
Risen to a holier state.[32]

If this revelation is an Easter vision, it's also a Christmas vision. Better, it's an Advent vision. As you noted, the arrival of Christ in the spirit world is explicitly called "the advent of the Son of God" in verse 16. Advent is the liturgical season spread over the four Sundays preceding Christmas, and I've noticed that it's become more familiar in Latter-day Saint homes. The word *advent* means "arrival" or "coming." Advent season, then, is a period of anticipation and reflection on the coming of Christ into the world, and its mood of expectant desire links Christians to the Jewish longing for the Messiah's arrival. It aptly captures the atmosphere of the "innumerable company of the spirits of the just" awaiting the coming of Christ in spirit prison (138:12).

The dead await an advent like the one I await and the one the Jewish faithful await—namely, the Savior's arrival in a world of darkness. The message of section 138, then, speaks directly to we who look for Christ's arrival today: we must wake from darkness, prepare ourselves, gather together, and attend to life's "first lessons" (138:56). What are these lessons? The text doesn't answer directly. My first lessons, the ones learned at my earthly parents' side and, I presume, from heavenly parents before that, are these: my life is a good gift I must give away, my selfishness is a prison I build for myself, my rescuer is Christ whom we await, and my labor is in his vineyard. Many churches celebrate a "Festival of Lessons and Carols" before Christmas, and it strikes me that this is just the mood of section 138: a festival of lessons and carols. I imagine the assembly singing the iconic Advent carol:

O come, O come, Emmanuel,
and ransom captive Israel

that mourns in lonely exile here
until the Son of God appear.

O come, O Branch of Jesse's stem,
unto your own and rescue them!
From depths of hell your people save,
and give them victory o'er the grave.[33]

If this is an Easter and Advent text, then certainly it is a millennial text! Section 138 is a kind of preperformance of the Second Coming. Take its narration of Christ's reception by the dead, put it in the future tense, and it sounds like it's straight from the end-times prophecies—the happier ones, anyway—of sections 45, 76, or 88 or the book of Revelation: "The saints [shall rejoice] in their redemption, and [shall bow] the knee and [acknowledge] the Son of God as their Redeemer and Deliverer from death and the chains of hell. Their countenances [will shine], and the radiance from the presence of the Lord [will rest] upon them, and they [will sing] praises unto his holy name" (138:23–24).

In its picture of Christ victoriously descending in glory, Joseph F. Smith's vision is like a preview of coming attractions for latter-day disciples. We likewise anticipate the coming of Christ into this world to free us from our chains and sow his radiance in our countenances. And so I think we can take Christ's actions in the spirit world as a bellwether of his actions in our world on that great and last day.

Try the same future-tense trick, this time projecting Christ's conduct in the spirit world onto his millennial reign: "Our Redeemer [will spend] his time during his sojourn in [our world], instructing and preparing the faithful . . . who [have] testified of him in the flesh; that they might carry the message of redemption unto *all* the [wicked], unto whom he [will not go] personally, because of their rebellion and transgression, that they through the ministration of his servants might also hear his words" (138:36–37, emphasis added).

The application of these verses is a hypothetical, of course, but I think it fits well with Restoration teachings about *how* the returning Savior will triumph over all enemies. Just as you've already found in section 76, Christ triumphs here not by sentencing the wicked to hell but by releasing them from its shackles. He refuses to accept any victory that ends in the defeat of his enemies. Christ's stubborn, relentless love pushes forward until his light reaches the darkest hell on earth. How is such a total victory to be achieved? Section 138 has the brilliant solution: to save his enemies, Christ enlists his friends. "Through the ministration of his servants," the rebellious and the transgressors will hear his words and may become "heirs of salvation" (138:37, 59).

> *Oh, how joyful it will be*
> *When our Savior we shall see!*
> *When in splendor he'll descend,*
> *Then all wickedness will end.*
>
> *Oh, what songs we then will sing*
> *To our Savior, Lord, and King!*
> *Oh, what love will then bear sway*
> *When our fears shall flee away!*[34]

Easter, Advent, and the Second Coming all compassed in sixty short verses! What these events share, of course, and what makes them so immediately relevant to section 138, is the celebration of Christ's presence. The Greek word *parousia* gathers up all these meanings and moods. *Parousia* means, simply, "presence, coming or arrival," and in the New Testament it names the presence of Christ. If you start reading the scriptures with an eye for the presence of Christ—whether in prophecy, narrative, or vision—you start to see that events and promises that once seemed unrelated now seem to share a lot in common.

Here's a small chorus of such passages that speak separately but harmoniously with section 138 of the *parousia*:

- Messianic prophecies in the Old Testament, including Isaiah's promise that "a virgin shall conceive, and bear a son, and shall call his name ['God with us']" (Isaiah 7:14).

- Premortal visions of Christ like the Savior's appearance to the brother of Jared, where he promises, "Even as I appear unto thee to be in the spirit will I appear unto my people in the flesh" (Ether 3:16).

- Joyful proclamations at the time of Jesus's birth, like Zachariah's exclamation, "Blessed be the Lord God of Israel; for he hath visited and redeemed his people" (Luke 1:68).

- Christ's own ministry, during which he taught that "the kingdom of God is [already] within you" (Luke 17:21).

- Postresurrection visitations including Christ's ministry among the Nephites, when the expectant multitude "saw a Man descending out of heaven; and he was clothed in a white robe; and he came down and stood in the midst of them" (3 Nephi 11:8).

- Latter-day visitations such as Christ's visit to the Kirtland temple, which we just read, and Joseph Smith's first vision, of which he wrote, "I saw two Personages, whose brightness and glory defy all description, standing above me in the air. One of them spake unto me, calling me by name and said, pointing to the other—*This is My Beloved Son. Hear Him!*" (Joseph Smith—History 1:16).

- Postmortal promises to Christ's people, like his reassurance to the Galilee disciples that "I am with you alway, even unto the end of the world" (Matthew 28:20) and his admonition to the early Saints to "be of good cheer . . . ; for I am in your midst, and I have not forsaken you" (Doctrine and Covenants 61:36).

Each of these moments is located at a different point in time and in space, each distant from Christ's first and second ministries to different degrees. And yet Christ is present in all of them. In fact, we begin to see that prophecies of the "first" and "second" comings were never meant to suggest that there were only to be two. In reality, if the record of the scriptures is to be believed, Christ offers his presence abundantly to his children in all times and in all places. The spiritual history of the world over the past two millennia is less like a long, dark night of divine absence strung between the sunset and sunrise of Christ's presence—the Ascension and the Second Coming—and more like a canopy of brilliant stars. Paraphrasing a philosopher we both love, any moment might open, for the worthy, like a door to the presence of Christ.[35]

I draw two lessons from placing section 138 in the larger context of the biblical *parousia*. First, the reality that Christ is present among his people in many times and places fits nicely with what I suggested about section 130: namely, that these visions of Christ lead us gently away from religious ideologies that would draw a strong arrow of time toward a score-settling Second Coming. Instead, we see that Christ comes among us often and comes with healing in his wings, not vengeance. As Sister Amy Wright said, and as you heard echoed in section 130, "Everything is going to be OK." Second, I take from these passages examples of the expectant posture to be assumed by those who await the imminent presence of Christ. Like the hosts of the dead described in section 138, we wait with alert preparedness, personal purity, hopeful patience, cheer in affliction, and obedient alacrity.

And one more thing as we approach the end of this project. When I put myself in the humble, expectant posture of one who awaits the *parousia*, I feel a time-traversing kinship with the hosts of the dead, the traumatized disciples at Bountiful, the young Joseph

Smith in a bare copse, Joseph and Sidney poring over the Bible, and Joseph and Oliver at the pulpit of the Kirtland temple. It's as if time folds in on itself and the presence of Christ passes through its layered thickness to align prophecy with its endless succession of fulfillments.

You point out the interlacing of section 138 with Luke 4, that electrifying scene in which Christ enters the Nazareth synagogue, mounts the bema, unrolls the great scroll of Isaiah, and reads to the assembled townspeople: "The Spirit of the Lord is upon me, because he hath anointed me to preach the gospel to the poor; he hath sent me to heal the brokenhearted, to preach deliverance to the captives, and recovering of sight to the blind, to set at liberty them that are bruised, to preach the acceptable year of the Lord" (Luke 4:18–19).

Something about his reading rivets the crowd. I have to imagine it's in the way he pronounces the word "me": the Spirit of the Lord is upon *me*, has sent *me* to preach deliverance to the captives. The people know this isn't a rote recitation of ancient formulas. This is happening, this is *live*.

He furls the scroll, hands it to the attendant, and takes his seat. Everybody stares at him.

He says, "This day is this scripture fulfilled in your ears" (Luke 4:21). Prophecy is made real, from the very moment the words leap from scroll to tongue.

This is one of my favorite passages of scripture, both for the dramatic artistry with which Luke orchestrates the suspense and narrative payoff and, of course, for the power with which it proclaims Christ as our teacher, healer, and liberator. Section 138 resembles Luke 4 in both the descriptive drama of its narrative and its echoes of Isaiah's messianic proclamation: "While this vast multitude waited and conversed, rejoicing in the hour of their deliverance from the chains of death, the Son of God appeared, *declaring liberty to the captives* who had been faithful" (138:18; emphasis added).

But what really thrills me about Luke 4 is the way it folds and wraps time in order to fulfill prophecy in real time, every time: "This day is this scripture fulfilled in your ears" (Luke 4:21). Jesus brings the words of Isaiah to life in his own flesh and breath, and the Nazareth villagers witness it all. Isaiah's words are fulfilled again in the same way in section 138, when Christ quotes them to the vast assembly of the dead languishing in spirit prison. Indeed, the prophecy is fulfilled over and over again, made real every time these words are given as proclamation and received as testimony of Jesus Christ. The written word, the uttered proclamation, and the broken-open heart work together to bring God into the present.

This is where we've arrived in our study of these seven shining visions of Christ. You've led us to a glimpse of what it means to dwell *in* and with Christ—and of his dwelling in us—right here and now in the physical world, embraced by the power and finitude of a divine materiality. And I've approached an understanding of revelation as the presence of Christ shot through time and carried forward by an ongoing chain of prophecy and fulfillment. These visions have "touched the eyes of our understandings" (Doctrine and Covenants 76:19) and shown us the brilliance of Christ in the sanctuary of the present moment.

After all the study and the insights and the understandings, of course, the crucial thing is to come unto Christ. Writing these letters and reading yours have fed my desire to know his face and find his presence. It's assured me that there is no bar to my beginning here and now. I hope it may have done the same for you.

The very thought of Jesus is sweet. To rest in his presence is sweeter far.

Rosalynde

— NOTES —

1. Russell M. Nelson, "Hear Him" (general conference address, April 2020).
2. Robert M. Daines, "Sir, We Would Like to See Jesus" (general conference address, October 2023).
3. Bonnie H. Cordon, "Come unto Christ and Don't Come Alone" (general conference address, October 2021).
4. Jeffrey R. Holland, "The Message, the Meaning, and the Multitude" (general conference address, October 2019).
5. "Historical Introduction" to Revelation, circa Summer 1829 [D&C 19], 39, The Joseph Smith Papers, accessed December 26, 2023, https://www.josephsmithpapers.org/paper-summary/revelation-circa-summer-1829-dc-19/1.
6. "If thou lovest me," the Lord emphasizes throughout the Doctrine and Covenants, "thou shalt serve me and keep all my commandments. And behold, thou wilt remember the poor, and consecrate of thy properties for their support" (Doctrine and Covenants 42:29–30).
7. Bible Dictionary, "Glory of the Lord, or of Jehovah," available at https://www.churchofjesuschrist.org/study/scriptures/bd/glory-of-the-lord?lang=eng.
8. Jeffrey R. Holland, "The Maxwell Legacy in the 21st Century," *Neal A. Maxwell Institute for Religious Scholarship 2018 Annual Report*, 12, available at https://mi.byu.edu/2018-annual-report/.
9. Russell M. Nelson, "The Gathering of Scattered Israel" (general conference address, October 2006).
10. See section header for Doctrine and Covenants 76.
11. Does this mean that section 76 articulates a "universalist" doctrine of salvation? This way of talking seems a poor fit to me, especially given how profoundly this revelation in particular—let alone the Doctrine and Covenants in general—bends and reframes the whole of Christianity's traditional cosmology and soteriology. For more on this question, see Fiona and Terryl Given's excellent book, *The Christ Who Heals* (Salt Lake City: Deseret Book, 2017).
12. "2859 Kolpos," *Strong's Concordance*, available at https://biblehub.com/greek/2859.htm.

13. Jeffrey R. Holland, "The Grandeur of God" (general conference address, October 2003). This theme is discussed in Robert M. Daines, "Sir, We Would Like to See Jesus" (general conference address, October 2023).

14. "The Family: A Proclamation to the World," Gospel Library, also available at https://www.churchofjesuschrist.org/study/scriptures/the-family-a-proclamation-to-the-world/the-family-a-proclamation-to-the-world?lang=eng.

15. Eliza R. Snow, "O My Father." This poem serves as the text for "O My Father," *Hymns*, no. 292.

16. Russell M. Nelson, "Salvation and Exaltation" (general conference address, April 2008).

17. See section header for Doctrine and Covenants 88.

18. "I Am a Child of God," *Hymns*, no. 301.

19. See Russell M. Nelson, "The Correct Name of the Church" (general conference address, October 2018).

20. Joan E. Taylor, *What Did Jesus Look Like?* (London: Bloomsbury T&T Clark, 2018).

21. Clement William Grene, "Review: What Did Jesus Look Like?," *Religion and Theology* 26, no. 1 (January 2019): 165–67.

22. "Jesus, the Very Thought of Thee," *Hymns*, no. 141.

23. Karl Ove Knausgaard, *My Struggle, Book 1* (New York: Farrar, Straus and Giroux, 2013), 21.

24. Dallin H. Oaks, in "Meaningful Scripture Study" (video), 2012, available at https://www.churchofjesuschrist.org/media/video/2013-02-1670-231-meaningful-scripture-study?lang=eng.

25. Steven C. Harper, *Making Sense of the Doctrine and Covenants: A Guided Tour through Modern Revelations* (Salt Lake City: Deseret Book, 2008), 474.

26. Minutes and Discourses, 6–7 April 1844, as published in *Times and Seasons*, p. 613, The Joseph Smith Papers, accessed November 3, 2023, https://www.josephsmithpapers.org/paper-summary/minutes-and-discourses-6-7-april-1844-as-published-in-times-and-seasons/11.

27. Harper, *Making Sense of the Doctrine and Covenants*, 474.

28. Amy A. Wright, "Abide the Day in Christ" (general conference address, October 2023).

29. Ronald E. Bartholomew, "The Textual Development of Doctrine and Covenants 130:22 and the Embodiment of the Holy Ghost," *BYU Studies Quarterly* 52, no. 3 (2013), available at https://scholarsarchive.byu.edu/byusq/vol52/iss3/2.

30. See Jeffrey R. Holland, "My Words . . . Never Cease" (general conference address, April 2008).

31. Harper, *Making Sense of the Doctrine and Covenants*, 508.

32. "He Is Risen!," *Hymns*, no. 199.

33. "O Come, O Come, Emmanuel," traditional hymn.

34. "Come, Ye Children of the Lord," *Hymns*, no. 58.

35. "For every second of time [is] the strait gate through which the Messiah might enter." Walter Benjamin, "Theses on the Philosophy of History." *Critical Theory and Society.* (New York: Routledge, 1989).

ABOUT THE AUTHORS

ROSALYNDE FRANDSEN WELCH is a research fellow and associate director at the Neal A. Maxwell Institute for Religious Scholarship at Brigham Young University. She holds a BA in English from BYU and a PhD in early modern English literature from the University of California San Diego. She is the author of numerous articles on Latter-day Saint theology and scripture. She is the author of two books, including, with Adam Miller, the Deseret Book publication *Seven Gospels: The Many Lives of Christ in the Book of Mormon.*

ADAM S. MILLER is a professor of philosophy at Collin College in McKinney, Texas. He earned a BA in comparative literature from Brigham Young University and an MA and PhD in philosophy from Villanova University. He is the author of more than a dozen books, including a number of other publications with Deseret Book, *Letters to a Young Mormon, An Early Resurrection, Original Grace,* and, with Rosalynde Welch, *Seven Gospels.* He also directs the Latter-day Saint Theology Seminar.